THE FINN EPISODE
IN BEOWULF

THE FINN EPISODE IN BEOWULF

An Essay in Interpretation

by

R. A. WILLIAMS, Ph.D., D.Litt.

PROFESSOR OF GERMAN AND TEUTONIC PHILOLOGY
AT THE QUEEN'S UNIVERSITY OF BELFAST

CAMBRIDGE

AT THE UNIVERSITY PRESS

MCMXXIV

CAMBRIDGE UNIVERSITY PRESS
Cambridge, New York, Melbourne, Madrid, Cape Town,
Singapore, São Paulo, Delhi, Tokyo, Mexico City

Cambridge University Press
The Edinburgh Building, Cambridge CB2 8RU, UK

Published in the United States of America by Cambridge University Press, New York

www.cambridge.org
Information on this title: www.cambridge.org/9781107600225

© Cambridge University Press 1926

First published 1926
First paperback edition 2011

A catalogue record for this publication is available from the British Library

ISBN 978-1-107-60022-5 Paperback

PREFACE

THE following Essay originated in studies devoted to the history of the Nibelungen Saga.

Boer's theory that this Saga was historically connected with the Finn Saga exerted a strong fascination on me, and I would willingly have believed it, if I could: there were however difficulties in the way. Of so much I was persuaded, namely, that there was a strong resemblance between the *second* part of the Nibelungen Saga and the Finn Saga, but I was by no means convinced that this *generic* relationship justified the inference of a *genetic* relationship. Before we could pose the problem of the latter in any form that would really promise the possibility of a solution, it seemed to me necessary to find some means of rendering the above-mentioned resemblance more definite and comprehensive than it appears in the transmitted texts. It suggested itself to me that this might possibly be accomplished by using the second part of the Nibelungen Saga in order to supplement the incomplete historical evidence for the Finn Saga: if, namely, the fragmentary content of the Finn Saga could in this way be reconstructed as a whole, it was clear that we should be in a better position to judge, firstly, just how close the relationship between it and the Nibelungen Saga was, and, secondly, to what extent this vindicated an enquiry into the possibility of a historical connection between the two.

Put to the test in the manner exemplified in Chapter IV of the following Essay, this process enabled me, without insuperable difficulty, to supply hypothetically the main missing elements of content in the Finn Saga. I was then faced by the problem of reconciling this reconstruction with the text of the Episode in *Beowulf*. I admit that for long I had not the courage to undertake this difficult task. It is true, I felt subjectively that the *Beowulf* text did admit of an interpretation in harmony with my reconstruction, but, alas, of one which differed at various important points from what had a claim to be regarded as at least the fashionable interpretation; and at first I saw no means of showing objectively that my subjective impression was right. Finally, however, it occurred to me that, the difficulties of the Episode being mainly those of ambiguity, there might be a possibility of solving them by means of the method I have outlined in the first chapter of the Essay. Disregarding, as far as in me lay, the reconstruction I had already made, I proceeded with the aid of this method to attempt a resolution of the ambiguities of the text. The method proved more fruitful than I had ventured to expect, and to my great pleasure the results gained harmonized fully with my reconstruction. Herein there seemed to be a guarantee that, in so far as I had really succeeded in applying the method objectively and without serious errors of detail, both my reconstruction and my interpretation were correct.

If my view of the content of the Finn Saga comes anywhere near to the truth, it would seem to justify raising the question, whether there could not have been a direct contact (not one at several removes, as Boer conceived) between the story of Finn and Hnæf and the story of Attila and the Burgundian princes which forms the second part of the Nibelungen Saga. I did not, however, venture to pose this problem with a view to its solution, so long as the preliminary steps, taken in my Essay, had not stood the fire of criticism. Of a searching examination I hope they will be found worthy, and even if the result were not to me encouraging, I should at any rate have cause for gratitude, if warned off a road that might lead far astray.

Throughout the Essay I have adopted the standpoint that the *Beowulf* is the work of one man. If it be necessary nowadays to excuse or defend my procedure, I can only say that, as a working hypothesis, this view seems to me altogether superior to the theory of composite workmanship. As far as I can judge, the latter presents us only with *disjecti membra poetae*, while the former holds forth at least the promise of closer acquaintance with the aims and methods—circumscribed, indeed, by local and temporal conditions—of a true poet. There may be contradictions in the Epic, but one can plead with Goethe:

Die Welt ist voller Widerspruch,
Und sollte sich's nicht widersprechen?

It did not seem necessary to lengthen my task by discussing the problems of interpretation raised by the text of the Finnsburg Fragment. Fortunately, the points at which the Fragment's restricted content throws light on the main problems of the Episode are quite clear. Once these are exhausted, there is probably more illumination to be gained for the Fragment from the standpoint of the Episode, than contrariwise.

It is a pleasure to acknowledge here the very great service rendered by my colleague, A. O. Belfour, Esq., who had the kindness to undertake the exacting task of reading a second proof, and to assist me with valuable observations.

R. A. WILLIAMS

BELFAST
August 1924

TABLE OF CONTENTS

KEY TO THE COMMENTARY

(CHAPTER TWO)

A

For the purposes of interpretation the text of the Episode is quoted in segments, as follows:

Lines	Page	Lines	Page	Lines	Page
1063–67	10	1089–94	56	1121 b–22 a	77
1068–70	12	1095–96 a	56	1125–27 a	78
1071–74 a	24	1096 b–97	59	1127 b–29 a	82
1076–79 a	34	1098–99 a	62	1129 b–31 a	88
1079 b–80 a	34	1099 b–1103	65	1131 b–36 a	89
1080 b–81	38	1104–06	66	1137 b–38 a	91
1082–83	39	1107–08 a	68	1140–41	91
1084–85 a	41	1113 b	73	1142–45	92
1085 b	47	1114–16	74	1146–1151 a	101
1086–87 a	52	1117–18	75	1151 b–52	103
1087 b–88	55				

B

ALPHABETICAL LIST OF WORDS AND PHRASES DISCUSSED

(Figures in brackets refer to lines of the text; others to pages in this Essay)

Ac (1085), 48f.; cp. 144ff.
arum heolde (1099), 63
astah (1118), 76f.
að (1107), 68, 70
aðum benemde (1097), 60

Bearm (1144), 93
bearnum (1074), 33; cp. 74
benemde (1097), 60
broðrum (1074), 33

Eaferum (1068), 12f., 19f., 21f.
eal gerymdon (1086), 54
earme on eaxle (1117), 75
elne unflitme (1097), 60, 83, 84 f.
Eotena (1072, 1088, 1141), 25, 29, 30, 55, 91, 92; cp. 139ff.
Eotenum (1145), 93, 98, 99

Feorum (1152), 103ff.
ferhð-frecan (1146), 102
Finnel (1128), 83ff.
forþringan (1084), 41ff., 47; cp. 166ff.
frecnan (1104), 67
freondum befeallen (1126), 82; cp. 20
Frysland geseon (1126), 79, 80
fundode (1137), 91

Geæfned (1107), 70
gefeohtan (1083), 39
gemænden (1101), 66
gemunde (1141), 91, 92
gerymdon (1086), 52, 54
gold (1107), 68ff.
guð-rinc astah (1118), 76f.

CHAPTER ONE

INTRODUCTION

IN the following Essay I have proceeded on the assumption that, in view of the very restricted nature of the historical evidence for the Finn Saga, the notorious difficulties presented to the interpreter by the Finn Episode in the epic of *Beowulf* are only capable of solution, if at all, through the rigid application of a unified critical method. The purpose of this Introduction is to explain the method I have adopted. I begin therefore by attempting to formulate as clearly as possible the nature of the difficulties referred to.

These difficulties may be put in two classes, external and nternal. To the first, the external class, I assign such obstacles as arise from the textual transmission—the text is of course unique and not above suspicion as to its reliability —from unusual words and idioms and the like linguistic minutiae. To the second I assign the difficulties caused by what it is usual to call somewhat indefinitely the "allusiveness" of the Episode, or to indicate by equally vague circumlocutions, such as "the allusive manner in which the story is told."

As regards the first class it may be claimed that they are not in themselves very alarming. They do not exceed the measure of what modern criticism in favourable circumstances may very satisfactorily explain, and certainly do not account for the fact that after many years of co-operative effort an agreed interpretation of the Episode has not yet been attained. We must suspect, therefore, that the second class of difficulties present the main obstacle in our attempts to solve the problem with which we are here concerned. Hence it seems to be advisable to examine what is connoted by speaking of the allusiveness of the Episode, or the allusive manner of its story-telling.

If we reflect that, strictly speaking, all employment of language is more or less allusive, it becomes evident that the epithet in this connection is not very enlightening. If we are telling a story, we can generally count on our audience having a certain amount of relevant knowledge which will render it unnecessary for us to state all the pertinent circumstances in so many definite propositions. Much can therefore be conveyed allusively, and we naturally tend to take advantage of the fact. It cannot consequently be merely the allusiveness of the Episode which puzzles us, but some attendant circumstance or some peculiar form of allusiveness, or both together. As a matter of fact it is both these things together.

The allusiveness in question is of a very concentrated kind, *i.e.* it does not go outside of the matter in hand; it is solely to personages and events contained in the story. That is obviously an allusiveness which the teller can only permit himself when the story is not a new one, when he reckons on its already being known to his audience. But the poet sang for his contemporaries, not for us, and we no longer know what was familiar to everybody in those days. The allusiveness therefore is attended by *our* ignorance. Again, it is the main events, a clear statement of which would be necessary to *us*, if we were immediately to grasp the story, which are conveyed thus allusively. That is to say, the poet is *not*, in the ordinary meaning of the word, *telling* a story, *i.e.* narrating a chain of happenings in the order in which they occurred. He is rather recalling to his hearers' minds well-known situations which could be conjured up by merely alluding to well-known events and personages. For certain purposes such indications would be much more effective than the repetition of an oft-told narrative, but on us, of course, the effect is largely lost. The situations cannot rise before our inward gaze until we have reconstructed the missing narrative from the very indications which once meant so much and now convey so little. It is true we hold the links of a chain in our hands, but how are they to be fitted together?

The question directs our attention to what is lacking in the indications from our point of view. A clear narrative would have presented to us the events and actors of the story not only completely, but in a definite order, and in their relations to one another and the whole of which they formed the parts. This completeness, order and interrelationship of the elements, which went without saying as far as the poet's audience was concerned, *we* have to supply. The task is rendered particularly difficult by the fact that the story deals with two sets of people and their mutual relationships. Much that is said about one might, for all we can see, be equally said about either. Indications which in any case it would not have been altogether easy to place in their temporal relations have thus in addition a highly puzzling ambiguity of reference. Not only have we to decide when in order of time particular actions were done, but also whether they originated with one or other of two parties, to either of which, for all we know, the actors might have belonged.

The difficulties occasioned by allusiveness do not however end here; they react in a serious way on the external factors of difficulty contained in the language of the text.

Language has of course a very general character of ambiguity —using that word in the sense either of a duality or plurality of meanings. Most words have more than one meaning, many have more than one function as different parts of speech; in addition we have the various figures of speech, metaphor, irony and so on, by which almost any word can be made to denote something quite different from its usual meaning. But although this can, and often does, give rise to misunderstandings on the part of the hearer, we are, generally speaking, not very conscious of ambiguity in what we hear or read. The evident reason of this is that, where a certain sympathy, a certain community of thought, feeling, interest, knowledge, exists between speaker and hearer (or author and reader), the formal ambiguity of language does not produce the effect which might be expected of it. The factors which govern this sympathy are obviously very complex and do not call for analysis here, but attention may be drawn to the circumstance that they are very largely of a concrete nature, and that these concrete factors principally regulate the perception of meaning conveyed in formally ambiguous terms. We can, I think, sum such factors up in the term "situation," using the word so as to include not only the surroundings and antecedents of speaker and hearer, but also whatever is concrete in the matter of discourse. In general, I believe, it can be claimed that the hearer perceives as the meaning of ambiguous words and phrases whatever among their possibilities of meaning is not contradicted by the situation. When there is complete sympathy between him and the speaker, the situation factors which regulate his perception of meaning can be conceived as congruent with those which regulate the speaker's choice of words, and misunderstandings can hardly arise. Wherever the sympathy is not complete this congruence will also be incomplete, and the possibility of misunderstanding is given. It should be noted, however, that misunderstanding does not necessarily lead to the perception of ambiguity. The hearer often perceives a possible, but not intended, meaning. He however holds this to be the meaning intended, and is not likely to notice that he is going wrong, until something occurs to draw his attention to the fact. The result is then often enough a "fight about words," the speaker holding what he originally said to be capable of only one meaning, that which he intended, and the hearer being equally convinced that only *his* meaning is possible. Often enough both sides are right in the sense that, without being aware of it, each has a different conception of the underlying situation, and neither allows for formal ambiguity in the statement made.

It follows from the above that in critically interpreting a written text the natural and rational manner of solving any ambiguities of utterance contained therein is by a reference to the situation connoted by the whole, since this enables us to reject any alternative meanings which are contradicted thereby. In so doing we may reckon either with our conception of the situation of the author at the time of composition or with the situation given along with the things and occurrences which are the subject of discourse—frequently of course our reasoning will proceed by combining both situations. In the less subjective styles of composition, *e.g.* epic or drama, the reference to the situation of the author will naturally have rather a subordinate importance, and we shall have to depend mainly on the internal situation of things presented by the author's matter.

With these considerations on the ambiguity of language in front of us, it is obvious that, when the situation given with the context of a text is ambiguous—as in many respects we noted it to be in the case of the Episode—the critic must have added difficulty in dealing with formal ambiguities in the text. Clearly, it is only when the situation is unambiguous that we can hope for an immediate resolution of formal ambiguities. We must reckon therefore among the difficulties occasioned by allusiveness any resultant uncertainty in dealing with formal ambiguity.

When we cannot solve ambiguities of fact by experiment we seek to rationalize them by an estimate of probability. The interpretation of the Episode is therefore carried out rationally by estimating the relative probability of different alternatives. The above analysis of the causes of difficulty has brought out that this calculation must embrace two parallel sets of factors presented by ambiguity both of language and situation. So far as the present writer is aware, no systematic attempt has, however, yet been made to deal with the interaction of both sets of factors. It has of late been customary to make full allowance for the ambiguities of situation, but the complexities introduced by the parallel ambiguities of language seem to have been largely disregarded. In this Essay the attempt is made to make due allowance for *both* sets of factors, and thus to supplement and, where possible and necessary, correct the results which have recently been attained by writers, who, like Chambers, Lawrence and Ayres, have demonstrated anew how important it is to take a full view of the situation as a whole, and weigh the various possibilities contained in it.

The novelty of the present venture consists therefore mainly in the fact that the writer has, to the best of his ability, consistently and persistently subjected himself to the effort to distinguish clearly in the language of the text between that which is ambiguous and that which is not. To carry this through effectively it was necessary, as far as possible, to draw a line between what might appear ambiguous to us, although it was not so in reality, and what really was ambiguous from the standpoint of former times. The argument has therefore led not only to insisting on formal ambiguities which have been ignored, but also in some cases to claiming as not ambiguous expressions which, generally by a sort of tacit consent, have been hitherto regarded as being so.

As regards the form of my Essay, the method adopted made it imperative that once more (to borrow a witty allusion from W. W. Lawrence) a rivulet of text should meander through a meadow of annotation; whereby it is left to the reader to decide whether "jungle" would not be nearer the mark than "meadow." In this, the main part of the Essay, I have aimed at such an exposition of the probabilities as would be progressive and cumulative, and thus lead to a unified result in the interpretation of the whole. While doing this I have tried to take into account that each separate passage of the Episode stands in an individual relationship to the situation. This, I believe, renders it necessary that there should be a fresh reckoning of probability made for each ambiguous passage, taking into account this individual relationship. Thus it is insufficient to show that a meaning, x, is the probable meaning of one ambiguous passage, and then to fix on one alternative meaning of another ambiguous passage because this particular alternative harmonizes with x—it is necessary to show in addition that the selected alternative not only harmonizes with x but is also not less probable than any other alternative, when the individual relationship of the passage to the situation is taken into account.

On the other hand, if we proceed by varied estimates of probability in the sense indicated, I think it can be claimed that, if these are properly performed, their correctness will show itself in the unforced harmony of the results. We must assume that the full situation as once known enabled the poet's contemporaries to reject unhesitatingly the unsuitable alternatives presented by formal ambiguity, *i.e.* the correct meaning was to them a certainty because there was nothing in the situation to contradict it. It follows from this that in our incomplete knowledge of the situation, so far as it is gathered from what is unambiguous in the historical evidence, and therefore agrees actually with a part of what was once known, there can be nothing to contradict the meaning that once was certain, but is conveyed to us in ambiguous terms. Hence what *was* certain must to us to-day (supposing, namely, what is in a large sense true, that any variations of literal meaning of most of the words used can be made out with approximate correctness) be capable of being shown either as certain, probable, or possible, when we take into account the situation; from which it follows that all meanings which can be *correctly* reckoned as probable will harmonize with each other, and with all that are certain.

I hold it to be a further requirement of method, which I have attempted to satisfy in the second part of my Essay, that the estimate of the relative probability of given alternatives of meaning should be based on the situation (using that word in the sense explained above, p. 4) *as given by the historical evidence*, and by that alone. There is a great temptation at such moments for us to simplify our task by introducing into the situation elements which are not given by the historical evidence, but might very possibly be contained in it, especially if, while assuming them to be there, we obtain an adequate explanation of the text. This temptation must in my opinion be resisted, as long as we are merely concerned with establishing what meaning is to be assigned to the language of the text. In ordinary life, I may remark, our instinctive attitude is to see in any adequate explanation of what we hear, the correct explanation. In the rough and tumble of human affairs we must rely on our intuition and abide by the consequences. Even for the critic it is very difficult to escape from this natural habit, but it is necessary to make the attempt.

On the other hand, once the meaning has been established in the manner indicated, it becomes advisable to test its reliability further, by examining whether the data thus obtained are capable of extension in order to supply such necessary elements of content as have been passed over by the author in silence. For this purpose, I conceive a different calculation of probabilities to be necessary, based on the comparison of the given content with other similar contents. This is explained and exemplified in the fourth chapter of the Essay. In the fifth chapter the whole results thus obtained are further tested by examining how far they enable us to grasp both the position of the Episode in the internal economy of the epic of *Beowulf*, and also its principle of composition.

With regard to the general tenor of Chapter Two, it has been my desire not so much to present original views as to weave into a continuous chain of demonstrative argument the unimpeachable results of the labour of my predecessors. If in many instances I have been compelled to differ from opinions which have a claim to be regarded as generally accepted, I hope it will be found that I have done so neither in a captious spirit nor for frivolous reasons, nor without due respect for the authority of scholars of established repute. For one thing I must crave the patience of the reader. The purposely discursive form of my comments, the necessity of constantly weighing different alternatives, led to a good deal of repetition of things that have already been said, and probably better said, by others. And in such a context the repetition of other people's observations may have a fatal appearance of their being brought forward as new and original. I might plead the time-worn excuse "Quod bene dictum est meum est," but will content myself with expressing the hope that wherever I have availed myself of the sword forged by another, I have not dishonoured the weapon by the use made of it. The demonstrative form of argument has, however, one advantage in that it reduces the necessity for polemics to a minimum. I have tried to realize this to the full by ignoring all expressions of opinion which were not real alternatives to the views I have defended and laboured by positive means to prove. Thus I have not discussed, for example, the recent effort of Imelmann to revive the theory that the story of Finn is a "Siedelungssage,"[1] because, if my interpretation of the Episode is correct, it is obvious that the Danes did *not* want to settle in Friesland—and so also in minor questions of exegesis.

In the first section of the following I have adopted on principle what may be described as a "Die-Hard" attitude as regards questions of textual criticism. In this field I take as my motto the following words of a famous critic:

Now, the plain duty of the humble interpreter is to see to it that the transmitted text be subjected to the closest possible cross-examination to make it yield whatever meaning it may have concealed so far.

KLAEBER in *Modern Philology*, III, 235.

The text is quoted in the main from Chambers' edition. Where I vary from this it is for reasons that will be apparent in the commentary.

[1] *Forschungen zur altenglischen Poesie*, Berlin, 1920, 342 ff.

CHAPTER TWO

INTERPRETATION OF THE EPISODE

1063   Þær wæs sang ond sweg   samod ætgædere
       fore Healfdenes   hilde-wisan,
       gomen-wudu greted,   gid oft wrecen;
       ðonne heal-gamen   Hroþgares scop
       æfter medo-bence   mænan scolde:

SUCH are the lines with which in *Beowulf* the famous digression known as the "Finn Episode" is introduced. They have not been accepted by critics of the text without demur. Difficulties have been raised regarding the correctness of the phrase in line 1064, and the question whether 1066–67 can be taken as a complete sentence. In my opinion such criticism is uncalled for. As a preliminary to the statement of my reasons it will be, however, advisable to recapitulate the situation with which these introductory lines deal.

It is the evening of the day after Beowulf's victory over Grendel. Hrothgar and his Danes are assembled in Heorot to celebrate their glorious release. The proceedings open with the ceremonious presentation by Hrothgar to Beowulf of rich rewards for his services, and we are told that Beowulf's companions also profited by the chieftain's generosity. Then song and rejoicing break forth, as denoted in the above lines, and Hrothgar's scop is called on to contribute something worthy of the occasion.

All day long, as was natural, men's minds had been full of Beowulf's exploit. In the morning the warriors returning from the mere, whither they had traced the flight of Grendel in the bloody tracks, had proclaimed his glory, and thinking of him as a stranger from a far land, had compared his expedition to Hrothgar's court with the famous *siðas* of eminent men like Sigemund and Heremod. Now in the evening, gathered together in Heorot, which still shows plain traces of the terrific struggle, they wonder whether in any other hall such a game had e'er been played as Beowulf played there with Grendel. Can any other hall compare with theirs as the scene of events so momentous? If so, they would like to hear of it.

ðonne heal-gamen Hroþgares scop…mænan scolde,

then was the scop to tell a tale of hall-play. And what follows contains a tale of hall-play! Finn's burg, red with the slaughter of its owners, furnishes a natural parallel to Heorot, even though there were no monsters busy in it.

In the situation as analyzed there is nothing to suggest that the exordium is incomplete, if, as some believe, the poet with line 1068 *Finnes eaferum ða hie se fær begeat* plunges *in medias res.* It is enough to have indicated that the subject proposed was to be *heal-gamen,* sport in hall, and that such an indication is provided in 1065–66, who can doubt, when we compare the introduction to the warrior's converse on the morning of the same day: *Ðær wæs Beowulfes mærðo mæned* (ll. 856 b–857 a)? The meaning of *mænan* is quite clear, it is "to talk about, to hold forth on" and, as we know from *Widsith, mænan fore mengo* was part of the office of a scop. It is quite impossible that *heal-gamen mænan* should mean "provide entertainment," as Clark Hall once translated; *heal-gamen* can only be an accusative of content. Nor is it difficult to believe that in this situation all the auditors asked, was that they should be told some story about hall-play. If they had confidence in their scop they could leave it to him to select a tale of the sort prescribed, one which would harmonize with their feelings on that great night in Heorot.

There is consequently no real reason to assume that *heal-gamen* by itself left the sense of *mænan* incomplete, and that it is therefore necessary to look for an exacter indication of the subject prescribed to the scop. It is, then, not very surprising that the efforts to supply this by emending the next line, though frequent, have not been very convincing; but of these more anon.

There still remains the difficulty of l. 1064. But is it a real difficulty? Many of the textual problems which have been raised in regard to *Beowulf* are more like excuses for emendations so-called than true problems. As regards the present one, two things are certain, firstly, that Hrothgar was Healfdene's son, secondly, that he was a famous war-leader. Is it now particularly surprising that Healfdene's son, the famous war-leader, should, by an assimilation of associations to which there are surely many parallels, become Healfdene's war-leader? To regard this as an anachronism is to view it from a modern standpoint. I venture to suggest that to a listener of those days *Healfdenes hilde-wisa* no more implied that Healfdene was alive, than *bearn Ecgþeowes* implied that Beowulf's father was alive.

> 1068   Finnes eaferum,   ða hie se fær begeat,
> hæleð Healf-Dena,   Hnæf Scyldinga,
> in Fres-wæle   feallan scolde.

The first of these lines presents a testing formal difficulty, namely, the syntax of *eaferum*, since a parallel construction to the dative with *feallan* seems to be lacking—and the most obvious attempt to deal with it, by assuming a so-called "instrumental" of the agent, is not satisfactory, in view of the fact that such a function for the dative in Anglo-Saxon is neither supported by clear evidence[1], nor, as far as I see, even to be made probable from what we know of the history of the language.

The opportunities for emendation at this place are very narrow; they leave us little choice but to telescope two sentences into one, of which the first as we have just seen is in sense complete and requires no improvement of this sort. That is not a promising circumstance, for it makes a considerable difference whether we are called on to join together two incomplete parts, or two parts of which one is complete

---

[1] This is my considered view in face of the arguments of Mr Green, see *Pub. of the Mod. Lang. Association of America*, xxxi, 769 ff. In any case, a dative of the agent would here be a monster since the agent of a verb in the active voice is of course the subject.

and the other—*seems* not to be so. Yet the only other alternative is that resigned protest of modern editors against the inconsiderate habits of ancient scribes: the assumption of a lacuna.

Of course, with the resources of modern criticism at our disposal it is not very difficult to make a suture by connecting *eaferum* with *mænan* in the preceding line, which can be accomplished in more than one way, either by supplying a preposition (*be* or *fram*) to govern *eaferum* or else by reading *eaferan* as accusative parallel to *heal-gamen* and assuming or not, as we please, an asyndetic jumble of *þa*-clauses to follow. If, however, we ask whether the sense thus arrived at is fully satisfactory, or whether in parallel passages introductory to a report there are in *Beowulf* examples of analogous constructions with verbs which imply speaking about a subject, the answer seems rather more than doubtful.

As regards the first point, the emendations put forward imply that not only the general subject but also the particular story illustrating it was prescribed to the bard by his listeners, *i.e.* he was given a subject and a title (or what amounted to one); it was to be a story of hall-sport, about Finn's sons (or as is popularly supposed, Finn's warriors). Against this I urge that the story which follows does not, properly speaking, deal with Finn's sons or warriors, neither the one nor the other coming in for anything but vague mention. I hold it to be improbable that the poet could have in his mind what he afterwards relates, and call it, or make others call it, by any such inadequate description. It is noticeable that modern writers refer to the Episode as a story of Finn, or of Hildeburh, or a "tragedy of Hengest," but as far as I have observed, never as the "Freswæl," though that would be an obvious title if the emendations and the popular translation of *eaferum* as "warriors" were really convincing[1].

---

[1] I admit that the scop's auditors *might* conceivably have asked for the story of the death of Finn's warriors; as I shall later try to demonstrate, the poet had, however, good grounds for not referring to this possibility (see below, pp. 130 ff).

The second of the questions just raised involves an important problem of style[1].

It is well known that the dialogue parts of *Beowulf* are generally introduced by phrases to which Heusler has given the generic name "kwath," further that the opening of the Finn Episode is exceptional in that here the kwath is lacking[2].

This only occurs in three other places, which differ in an important respect from the present, namely in this, that in all three instances (2518, 2813, 3110–14) the person speaking has already been speaking and after an interruption continues to do so. Now in these other cases a kwath is dropped for an obvious reason; we may argue therefore that it is not dropped by mere accident in the present case.

In these other cases the remark which interrupts the speech contains however a verb which implies speaking, and therefore serves *faute de mieux* to introduce the continuation, thus 2812, *het hyne brucan well:* "*þu eart...*," *i.e.* "told him to use it well, saying...." In ll. 1063–68 we have the same implication in *gid oft wrecen*, and *mænan scolde*.

The three cases just mentioned are all examples of direct report. They therefore stand in contrast with the rule which has been formulated by Klaeber[3], according to which a speech reported in indirect discourse must be preceded by *(ge)cwæð*, "following a preparatory statement of a more general character." As Klaeber's examples show, in such cases the indirect report is introduced by a formula in which a verb *implying* and one *denoting* the act of speaking are paired together. Since this rule is not followed here, we can argue that the report of the scop's song is intended by the poet as a direct report of the words actually used by the scop. This is confirmed by ll. 1159 *b*–60 *a*, *Leoð wæs asungen, gleomannes gyd*, which indicate that the delivery of the Episode was represented as part of the action of the poem, *i.e.* that

---

[1] This has already been treated at length by Green, *loc. cit.*, who comes to the same result as I do. As I cannot, however, accept his premisses I am forced to reopen the matter.

[2] *Z. f. d. A.* XLVI, 245.

[3] *Modern Philology*, III, 245.

what precedes is a quotation of words supposed actually to have been used in the situation described.

The rule for *Beowulf*, therefore, seems to be that a speech whether reported directly or indirectly must be introduced by a verb denoting the act of speaking (*e.g. maðelian, cweðan, secgan, sprecan, frignan*), but this "kwath" need not be repeated in taking up a directly reported speech again after an interruption. We have therefore still to explain why the kwath could be dropped in the opening lines of the Finn Episode although there was no interruption.

To accomplish this object it will be necessary for me first to define my attitude to the question whether the Episode represents a real lay or not. Most people seem to assume that it is only an abridgement, abstract or paraphrase of such, but this has been denied by Green[1], and the point must still, I think, be regarded as arguable.

The poet counted on his auditors having a detailed knowledge of the Finn Saga. This could only have been derived from a source that was much more complete than the Episode itself. Such source would in the circumstances of the times be certainly a poetical one, *i.e.* either a lay dealing with the whole saga, or a number of lays dealing with the different episodes and supplementing each other. We have, therefore, the following alternative possibilities:

(*a*) The Episode is an abstract of either a longer complete lay, or the contents of a number of lays.

(*b*) The Episode is a reproduction of a short lay on the whole Saga, in which the author had taken advantage of the fact that the story was already well known through oral tradition, in order to tell it for his own purposes in a very concise and allusive manner.

(*c*) The Episode is an adaptation of a lay such as that in (*b*).

Of these three possibilities I believe we can eliminate (*b*). The author of such a lay would have in view an audience which would be differentiated from the audience of the *Beowulf* poet by the fact that its attention was not concen-

[1] *Pub. Mod. Lang. Ass. of America*, xxxi, 782.

trated on a long epic poem. He would tell the story therefore in a manner, which, however concise and allusive, would not be adapted to the purposes of the *Beowulf* poet, and the latter, even if he knew such a lay, would not be able to transfer it unaltered into his epic[1]. We can say therefore this much, that the Episode is either an abstract in the sense of (*a*) above, or it is the adaptation of an original short lay, borrowing the grouping of events and characters from this, but treating the whole in a tone and manner adapted to the epic context in which it is an interlude. With that we may rest content, for it is probably hardly necessary to decide whether the Episode was an abstract, or the adaptation of what was in effect already an abstract, though made by someone else for different purposes. As, however, we have eliminated (*b*), it is plain that our poet is here guilty of an innocent imposture. He gives himself the air of reproducing the lay declaimed by Hrothgar's scop, but what he puts in the mouth of the latter is not a real lay, such as would in truth have been delivered by a scop under the circumstances depicted. It is something like that, but made for the poet's audience, not for the scop's.

The matter of the Finn Saga as a whole is rich in events and complex in structure. Obviously it could not lend itself easily to treatment in a digression such as was dictated by the economy of the epic of *Beowulf*. A great effort of compression was necessary in order to keep it from overflowing the limits thus prescribed. Even if by a lucky chance this effort had already been successfully made for other purposes by a predecessor from whom our poet could borrow to a greater or less extent, the Episode would still as a whole be subject in a special degree to the resultant necessity for extreme concision of statement and economy of the means of expression. This argument is not adversely affected by Heusler's undoubtedly correct assertion that the author "nicht blos kürzt,

---

[1] Of course I assume here that there is an organic relation between the Episode and the whole epic. That seems to me a necessary assumption, though perhaps not made by all. On the nature of this relation see below, Chapter v of this Essay.

sondern auch elegisch erweitert."[1] Even though at certain points, for example, in describing the scene at the pyre, the content is expanded descriptively in the interest of the elegiac effect aimed at, this obviously entailed a still more vigorous application of the contracting process to the actual narrative, in order to keep the whole story of the Saga within the bounds of ninety-one and a half alliterative lines.

In spite of this "elegiac expansion" of certain elements the Episode is a hurried affair. It had to be; for treated with the *Beowulf* poet's ordinary breadth of manner, the Finn Saga would have offered matter enough for another long epic. And it is by contrast with this, his usual manner, not merely by the rapidity with which images of action are made to flit before our gaze, that we instinctively feel how the poet has quickened his gait, to lead us almost breathlessly through a side alley. It does not here much matter whether the poet had learnt the secret of this rapid motion from others, or whether he evolved it for himself under the pressure of his necessity as a digressor from the main path of his epic. What is now of importance, is to note that this increased speed of movement reflects the effort of compression necessarily applied to the matter of the Saga.

We may well expect to find this reflected in the language used, and I consider that we have herein a principle which the interpreter must not neglect wherever it may be relevant. It is probable that we have already had an illustration of the applicability of this principle in the process by which *Healfdenes sunu, se mæra hilde-wisa* became *Healfdenes hilde-wisa*. It is probable that we have a further instance in the dropping of the "kwath." The poet has been narrating in his usual easy manner the ceremonies attendant on Hrothgar's presentation of rewards to Beowulf. He turns now to another matter, the symposium of song and speech which ensued. Quite abruptly he singles out the scop as the principal figure, and almost before we realize it we are plunged into the scop's story. We are only told that this person was called on to recite and it is

---

[1] *Lied und Epos*, p. 11.

left to us to infer that he did recite. It is an easy inference, but in other cases where a speaker is introduced with his speech as part of the action we are not required to make even that simple effort.

I think, therefore, we may conclude that at this point the poet was economical of language beyond his wont and for good cause, namely, because his task for the time being lay aside from his principal business and had to be performed expeditiously. I conceive also that we can hence derive light on the question of the suture, which we have still to solve. If, namely, it be conceded that the poet had reason to economize by dropping the otherwise usual "kwath," i.e. by leaving out an element in the ordinary structure of the introduction to a speech, it seems hardly likely that he would sacrifice the saving thus obtained, in order to dilate on the subject of the speech. Heusler has shown[1] that the "kwath" was by no means an otiose ornament, but had certain definite functions organic to the purpose of narrative. Among these was that of instructing the hearer on "inhalt oder art der nachfolgenden rede." Now if the "kwath" was here felt by the poet in spite of his usual custom to be dispensable, he must likewise have felt that its functions could be done without. He cannot, therefore, have deemed it necessary to go into details about the subject already indicated by the word *heal-gamen*, and the emendations criticized above must in consequence be considered as irrelevant.

The line of argument so far pursued tends to show that those editors who begin the report of the Finn Saga with l. 1068 are in the right. Stylistically speaking, they are not wrong, and from the methodical point of view they are well advised to abide by the historically attested *eaferum*. This presents indeed difficulties of its own, but for these the attempts at emendation have only substituted further difficulties, all the less pleasing because they spring not from fact but from hypothesis. On the whole it is better to explain *eaferum* than to explain it away.

[1] *Loc. cit.* p. 257.

I have claimed above that the composition of the Episode stands under the compulsion of a superior principle, the effort of condensation, and have sought to show that this gives us a means of dealing with certain difficulties. It is worth while to consider whether the same principle cannot be applied to explain the syntax of *eaferum*. For this is not the only unexpected dative of the Episode. A little further on we have *Hengeste* dependent on *gefeohtan*, a cause of much tribulation to the critics before it was judged well to leave it as it stands. And *Hengeste* takes the place of the more usual *wið Hengeste*, an analytic construction.

Now in O.E. it was of course possible at times to express by case-forms alone relations which could also be expressed by means of prepositions. Thus it was possible to say *þreate faran* instead of *mid þreate faran*. It is, historically speaking, clear that such constructions without preposition are survivals from an older stage of expression in which case-forms by themselves discharged functions which later were expressed more analytically. But in the progress from the older synthetic to the later analytic modes there must have been a transitional period when synthetic forms stood side by side with analytic, though usage was tending towards the latter. Gradually the synthetic forms would be eliminated, or where they were preserved be limited in their applicability. But since elimination was at work, a limited usage of the synthetic form in later days would argue a preceding more comprehensive usage in earlier times. And the memory of this more comprehensive usage would survive for a time, even when it had become so unusual as to have practically no place in the consciously careful style of the preserved literary monuments.

The comitative dative as in *þreate faran* seems to be limited in literary usage to the employment with verbs of motion and *wesan*, but it may very well have once been possible with intransitive verbs in general, to denote the participation of others as well as the subject in the action of the verb. Now the synthetic, in comparison with the analytic, is always a condensed mode of expression.

The poet leaps at a bound into the middle of his story, to the point at which the first struggle is over and the Danes have to mourn the loss of their leader, the Frisians of their princes, the sons of Finn[1]. To recall this situation to his auditors he has to remind them that both Hnæf and Finn's sons are fallen. But the fall of Hnæf is to him the more important event. It naturally presses into his consciousness with a greater intensity, and the death of the princes is subordinated as the accompanying circumstance, also of importance but in a lesser degree. He has therefore to say "Hnæf fell, and Finn's sons as well." A comitative dative, if at all possible, would obviously do the work very neatly and economically! I propose, therefore, to translate "With the sons of Finn, when the sudden calamity overtook them.... Hnæf was fated to fall." That is to say, Hnæf's fate was the same as that of the sons of Finn, the disaster which overwhelmed them was the cause also of his undoing. There is some support for the view of *eaferum* just advanced in the circumstance that the same explanation is applicable to the dative in phrases like *freondum befeallen, eorlum bedroren*. Delbrück's explanation[2] that "die Freunde das ausdrücken, womit, wodurch, woran der Fall erfolgt" strikes me as purely verbal. Since falling is a concrete idea there must here be an underlying image which is at the same time a metaphor for something else. Now a chieftain, say, who had been deprived of the support of his "friends" through their death in battle, could easily be conceived as "fallen from his high estate," and since the friends whose loss occasioned his "fall" were likewise "fallen," the assimilation of the two nuances of the same idea might easily result in the image that the prince was fallen "along with" his friends, *i.e.* accompanied them in their fall. The phrase would then be a natural result of the effort to express in a concrete way the abstract idea of privation[3].

[1] That "sons" is the necessary meaning of *eaferum* I shall immediately try to show.   [2] *Synkretismus*, p. 25.

[3] Comparable as regards the relation (though this is expressed analytically) and the underlying metaphor (though this expresses a different

Regarding the meaning of *eaferum*, it is usual to accept it as ambiguous. In spite of the high authority of Cosijn and his followers it is, however, very doubtful whether any other meaning than "son" can be assigned to it with a decent degree of probability. In *Beowulf* there are only two passages in which it does not certainly mean "son," namely this and l. 1710. But even in l. 1710 we can translate "son" without disturbing the sense. *Ar-Scyldingum*, the apposition to *eaferum*, is ambiguous; it might mean either the representatives of the dynasty or the people and the dynasty as a whole. We are not forced to take it in the latter sense here because such compounds usually refer to the folk and the dynasty, obviously on the principle of putting the representatives for the whole they stand for. As a matter of fact it is more likely that the apposition proves that the *Ar-Scyldingas* could be used of the dynasty alone, than that *eafora* could be used in the sense of vassal. And what little we know of Heremod does not prove that he could not have been a worry to the sons of Ecgwela. It is also possible that there is a climax, that the thought is "Heremod was a torment to the sons of Ecgwela and (consequently) a cause of the slaughter of his own and their people." The allusion is introduced to enforce the virtue of loyalty which Hrothgar is impressing on Beowulf. But a man's loyalty may be conceived in the first place as loyalty to the rulers, and through them to the people, and this conception was a likely one in those days—it is really the underlying conception of the comitatus.

Outside of *Beowulf* I can with the assistance of the *Sprachschatz* discover only one passage where *eafora* may have the meaning of vassal or retainer, viz. *Gen.* 2133 *b*. The *Sodoma ealdor*, already described as *eorlum bedroren, freonda feasceaft, secgum befylled*, here says to Abraham, *Eaforan syndon deade, folcgesiðas, nymðe fea ane, þe me mid sceoldon mearce healdan*. But on the principle of the part for the whole, the king of Sodom may be only emphasizing his loss

nuance of separation) are Mod. German, "mit einem Freunde zerfallen sein," and Mod. English, "to fall out with a friend."

by a reference to the point at which it touches him most nearly, namely the death of his sons. In any case the patriarchal relationships of the Old Testament would be bound to present difficulties in adapting to them the traditional terminology of Teutonic social organization and the meaning of *eafora* might in consequence experience an (apparent?) extension which would not otherwise be possible[1]. Apart from this example, even in Christian poetry *eafora* usually means "son" and is only occasionally employed as a synonym for *bearn* in the meaning of *descendant*, not retainer. Thus in *Genesis* (4 times), *Guthlac*, *Juliana*, *Phoenix* (each once) I find the descendants of Adam called *eaferan*. There is one such reference in *Genesis* (l. 2210) to Abraham's, one in *Daniel* (l. 672) to Nebuchadnezzar's descendants. We also meet with *monna eaforan* in *Gen.* 1251. When we consider the relative paucity of such cases, we can only conclude that the use of *eafora* in any meaning but "son" was less likely to be a result of the sense suggested as original by its etymology than the influence of Biblical phraseology. The possibility that *eafora* in *Beowulf* anywhere means "retainer" or "warrior," therefore, must appear exceedingly small.

Before we consider the meaning of ll. 1068–70 to be settled we have, however, still to consider a difficulty raised by the grammatically ambiguous *hæleð* in l. 1069, which may be either singular or plural. It is not of course of any great importance whether we have to understand that *the* hero of the Half-Danes, Hnæf, was killed, or that certain heroes of the Half-Danes, including Hnæf, were killed. If *one* fell it is pretty certain that he was not the only one. But if *hæleð* be plural it argues the possibility that the *hie* of the preceding half-line refers (proleptically) to it and not to *eaferum*. This raises the important question whether the sudden danger was one that befel the Danes or the Frisians. In the situation there is nothing to decide, so far as we know it. We do indeed hear

---

[1] The natural tendency would be to equate the *family* of a patriarch with the comitatus of a Teutonic prince, and the result would be that "son" and "retainer" would become equivalent terms.

of a sudden danger which overtook Finn at the end of the story (ll. 1146–47), and it has been held[1] that the reference here is to that concluding event. Since, however, the poet concentrates all his attention at the end on Finn[2], it seems extremely unlikely that he would refer by anticipation to this final catastrophe merely as one which befel Finn's sons. There is nothing for it, then, but to conclude that the *fær* occurred much earlier, and we must therefore suspect that it was the opening act of the hostilities between the two parties. But of which party first attacked the other we have no hint, *unless* it be in the passage under consideration, which means, that we have nothing to go on, unless we can solve the formal ambiguity without reference to the situation. The question therefore becomes, whether on general grounds it is more likely, or not, that the pronoun has a proleptic reference.

The proleptic use of the pronoun is fairly common in *Beowulf*[3]. On the other hand it may be argued that this proleptic use is only occasional, and can hardly be assumed as present, except when there is no other way of making satisfactory sense. Where we have equal choice between the usual and the occasional construction, it must, I think, be allowed that the probability is in favour of the non-occasional. In addition it seems pretty clear from Klaeber's examples that this proleptic use of the pronoun tends to be limited to principal sentences. In only two of his examples does the pronoun stand in a dependent sentence, and in one of these (l. 1674) it really points both ways. This would increase the chances against the proleptic use here. We are justified, therefore, in concluding that, while there is grammatically speaking a possibility that the poet expressed himself thus: "With the sons of Finn, when sudden danger overtook them (namely) the heroes of the Half-Danes," on the whole it is more likely he did not so express himself. In other words,

---

[1] *E.g.* by Lawrence, *Publ. of the Mod. Lang. Ass. of America*, xxx, 399, followed by Ayres, *Journ. Eng. and G. Phil.* xvi, 284, 290.

[2] Cp. below, p. 106.

[3] Cp. Klaeber, *Modern Philology*, iii, 255.

a reconstruction of the events of the story which made of this *fær* one that overtook the sons of Finn and therefore allowed us to deduce from it the *usual* syntactical relation of the pronoun, would, other things being equal, be preferable to one which made the *fær* overtake the Danes and forced us thus to deduce from it the merely occasional construction of such words.

It hardly seems necessary to permit ourselves to be puzzled by the relationships denoted in l. 1069, although superficial difficulties are presented by the fact that Hnæf, as we know from *Widsith*, was prince of the Hocings, while his men appear in the Episode both as Half-Danes and Danes. Since Beowulf in l. 1563 is called *freca Scyldinga* although he is a Geat, *Hnæf Scyldinga* does not necessarily point to a very close connection between the Hocings and the Danes. Hnæf may very well have been an "auswärtiger Gefolgsmann"[1] of the Scyldings. The Hocings may then be Half-Danes in the sense that though not Danish by descent, they are so by allegiance. By contrast with the Frisians they may then become Danes (l. 1090). Is it too fanciful to suppose that Hrothgar's father may have been called Healf-Dene out of compliment to such Half-Danes? According to Bugge[2] Healf-Dene denotes mixed descent. This may well have been so, but not necessarily to the exclusion of other motives. And indeed that a king of the Danes should wish to designate his son as a mongrel, does not seem a very satisfactory explanation, whereas he might consider it politic to call him Half-Dane, if that was understandable as a compliment to his allies without conveying any reflection about descent. Possibly also the concession of the right to allies to call themselves or be called Half-Danes would be felt as complimentary.

> 1071 Ne huru Hildeburh   herian þorfte
> Eotena treowe;   unsynnum wearð
> beloren leofum   æt þam lind-plegan,
> bearnum ond broðrum;

The first sentence of this (to *treowe*) presents us with perhaps the most troublesome crux in the Episode, since it

---

[1] Cp. Neckel, *PBB.* XLI, 422 ff.   [2] *PBB.* XII, 29.

contains no less than five separate ambiguities. Of these three are formal, since firstly the whole sentence is ambiguous (not generally recognized, but I shall try to prove it immediately); secondly, *eotena* may be the genitive plural either of *eoton* or *Éote*; and thirdly, *treowe* may denote either personal loyalty or loyalty between peoples. The other two arise from the situation; it does not appear to which side either Hildeburh or the group denoted by *eotena* is related.

Of these five I shall leave two out of the present discussion, namely, Hildeburh's relationship and the formal ambiguity of *eotena*. It may be taken as a firm result of criticism that Hildeburh is Finn's wife, Hnæf's sister and the *Hoces dohtor* of l. 1076 as well as the *cwen* of l. 1153. Equally it may be taken as established that the *eotena* are the same group as in ll. 1088, 1141 and 1145, and that they do not stand outside the two complexes of Frisians and Danes as a third independent party, but belong to one side or the other. The open questions regarding them are the meaning of their name (giants or Jutes?) and *which* of the sides they belong to. Of these the first has never been shown to have any real bearing on the story and is reserved therefore for discussion in an Appendix[1], since I hold that the content of the Episode can be elucidated quite as comfortably without deciding it. [It is probably of no more importance to the poet whether he refers to one of the contesting parties as *eotena* or *Fresna* (or *Healf-Dene*) than it is of importance whether a North British regiment in the English army be referred to as Highlanders or Scots or Sandies.] For the present, therefore, I take *eotena* as a group designation whose exact meaning can be neglected in the same way as we neglect the exact meaning of *Dene*, say, because it is not necessary to know it in order to make out the story. The really important problems of the present passage are indicated by the ambiguity of the sentence-form and the reference of *eotena* and, in a minor degree, the above-noted ambiguity of meaning in *treowe*, and to these I now address myself. I have first of all to show that the whole

[1] See below, pp. 139 ff.

sentence is ambiguous since this is often overlooked, and this I shall try to demonstrate as follows:

Negation[1] can be expressed by particles of varying function exemplified by the examples *No man*, *is not*, *untrue*. Grammatically speaking we are apt to lump together as negative all sentences into which these types of negation enter. Logically speaking, however, sentences like "No man would do it" or "That is untrue" are not negative but affirmative. The only sort of sentence which is formally a true negative is one like "That isn't true," *i.e.* in which negation is denoted by a negative particle modifying a finite verb. It is pretty plain that in this case we do not feel the negative particle as negating the idea expressed as predicate, but as negating a relation between that idea and the proposed subject[2]. The truly negative sentence in this sense may be represented by the formula familiar to logicians as "*A* is-not *B*." That is to say the only function *which corresponds to its form* is that of eliminating as a whole the affirmative proposition "*A* is *B*." In other words the only meaning explicit in the sentence "John isn't here" is one which can be denoted by "The assertion that John is here is false."

It is obvious that in the ordinary use of speech the functions of the negative sentence go beyond that of merely eliminating the corresponding positive. These further functions may be derived not from the meaning which is explicit in its form but from others that are implicit. The proposition "*A* is-not *B*" is valid for two cases, namely, when either *A* is not or *A* is not-*B*, *e.g.* "John was not loyal" is valid when either no such person existed or he was disloyal. When, therefore, the speaker has either of these cases in his mind he is justified in using the negative form of sentence, *i.e.* in denying formally the proposition "*A* is *B*." In so doing, however, he will feel that he is, as it were, challenging the hearer to infer the ground on which he makes the above denial, and he may

[1] For the logical aspect of this idea cp. W. E. Johnson, *Logic* (Cambridge, 1921), Part I, ch. v.

[2] Cp. Jespersen, *Negation*, ch. v.

therefore use the negative sentence for this purpose, a procedure which will be effective whenever the circumstances are favourable, *i.e.* when what has been already said or the surroundings help the hearer to reconstruct what is likely to have been in the speaker's mind. Now the impulse to deny *in toto* that A is B has not often to be satisfied relatively speaking. On the other hand the need for an alternative way of saying either "A is not" or "A is not-B" often makes itself felt. It is not surprising, therefore, that the negative sentence is more frequently used for what it implies than for what it explicitly states (cp. "He will not breathe again" as equivalent for "He has ceased to exist, he is dead" and the equivalence in ordinary use of "That isn't true," "That is untrue").

Before turning to apply the above remarks to the interpretation of *Beowulf* l. 1071, we must first take into consideration that for a sentence containing a verb plus a noun which denotes the aim of the activity the simple formula "A is B" must be extended to "A is B to C," that in consequence the validity of the corresponding negative sentence depends not only on the two alternative conditions mentioned above but also on a further one, viz. "C is not." Thus "Tell did not assassinate Gessner" would be valid if *either* Tell or Gessner did not exist. Hence the *Beowulf* sentence may *a priori* admit any one of *three* implications.

What may be called the *ne thearf* formula is fairly common in *Beowulf* and is obviously used to convey implications of the types just described. Its function is to indicate that a mental state or attitude expressed or typified by the dependent infinitive is excluded by circumstances, because either

(*a*) there is no one to feel so-and-so, *e.g.* ll. 2363 ff. "The Franks who met Beowulf on the field hadn't occasion to be boastful," because none of them (*lyt* in l. 2365 is of course litotes) survived; or,

(*b*) there is no object for a certain feeling, *e.g.* l. 1674 *b*, "thou wilt not have occasion to dread (what will no longer exist) murderous attacks from that quarter"; or,

(c) a positive cause eliminates a certain feeling, *e.g.* 1026 *b*,
"Beowulf hadn't occasion to be ashamed of the costly
gifts."

Before we proceed further with the application of these
remarks, it is advisable to make a distinction between what
may be called the serious and the ironical use of the negative
sentence, the latter coming under the head of the figure
known as litotes. Just as the negative phrase "not bad" may
suggest either "fair, middling" or (by litotes) "good, very
good," so the negative sentence may merely eliminate a
possibility, or permit us to infer the opposite of that possibility. Thus "I did not praise him" may convey "I refrained
from praising him (even though he was praiseworthy)" or it
may convey "I did the opposite, I blamed him." Litotes may
often be assumed for the *ne thearf* formula; thus, the example
quoted above under (c) plainly means "Beowulf had reason
to be proud of the gifts he received." But in a case like 2493 *b*
(There was not any need for him to seek a worse champion,
sc. than I) the privative statement is as strong as any positive,
i.e. we have circumlocution not understatement (= he was
satisfied that I was the best). Likely enough no litotes was
felt by the poet where occasionally it seems clear enough to
modern feeling. For example, l. 2873, *Nealles folc-cyning
fyrd-gesteallum gylpan þorfte*, suggests to us "The king had
reason to be ashamed of his companions-at-arms," but it may
well appear doubtful whether men of those days would have
connected any idea of shame with the prince—not he, but the
cowards themselves had reason to feel shame—while on the
other hand the statement that he had been deprived of the
opportunity to boast of his friends' support, which he had
earned by his munificence, must in itself have been a bitter
taunt to those who listened to Wiglaf's speech. The implication is therefore not that the king was ashamed, but that he
stood alone in the fight, being deprived of his natural
support.

Of the three formal possibilities of implication offered by
l. 1071 we must of course immediately eliminate one, viz.

"Hildeburh was not." There remains, therefore, the choice between the litotes "Hildeburh had not occasion to praise (what did not appear) the loyalty of the Eotens, *i.e.* she had reason to execrate their treachery," and the merely privative "Hildeburh had reason to refrain from praising the loyalty of the Eotens."

The popular interpretation, of course, is strongly in favour of the litotes. It should be noted, however, that it is supported only by the negative ground that there is nothing to contradict it. It is possible for l. 1071 to have the meaning usually postulated; it is possible that the poet wished to bring out that Hildeburh who had lost both sons and brothers had therein a special reason over and above merely general grounds to be indignant at someone's treachery; it is possible that treachery was the original cause of all the pother at Finn's court; it is possible that the poet desired to fix the war-guilt on one side or the other and was content to do this in a vaguely allusive way (which would doubtless be clear enough to his audience)—but for all these possibilities there is no direct evidence in the historical documents of the story, viz. the Episode and the Fragment. On the other hand, in the absence of direct evidence to the contrary it is equally possible with the foregoing (1) that l. 1071 means only that Hildeburh could not admire the loyalty of the Eotens; (2) that the poet wished to emphasize the depth of her sorrow for the dead by insisting that it prevented a feeling which would otherwise have been natural to her; (3) that the quarrel at Finn's burg was brought about accidentally, without treachery on either side; (4) that the poet was indifferent to the question of who was the guilty party, may even have considered that no guilt attached to either side. Furthermore, while there is no direct evidence that *treachery* was ascribed in the story to either side, there *is* direct evidence that this story contained a conspicuous example of loyalty. The Fragment shows that Hnæf's followers set a lofty example of true service to a chieftain in difficult circumstances (ll. 39 ff.). Combining the ambiguity of the whole sentence with the ambiguity of the reference in the name *Eotena* we have now a choice between four alternative possibilities, as follows:

(1) On the assumption of litotes the sentence may contain an allusion to treachery on the Frisian side.

(2) On the same assumption it may contain an allusion to treachery on the Danish side.

(3) On the assumption that the sentence is merely privative it may contain an allusion to the loyalty of the Frisians.

(4) On the same assumption as in (3) it may contain an allusion to the loyalty of the Danes.

Of the first three of these we can say that they are neither contradicted nor supported by the documentary evidence. Of the fourth we can say that it is *not* contradicted and *is* supported by the documentary evidence. In seeking to estimate the relative force of these facts we must bear in mind that the testimony of the Fragment makes it certain that the Danes' loyalty was a conspicuous element in one version of the story. On the other hand, no such datum makes it certain that treachery on either side or Frisian loyalty was conspicuous in any version. It is true these things *may* have been mentioned in versions that are lost or even in the missing parts which formed a whole with the Fragment, but it is our business to construct the story not from evidence which may once have existed but from that which we actually have. We can, indeed, only transfer the loyalty of the Danes from the Fragment to the Episode hypothetically, but a hypothesis which thus operates with a concrete datum is, if other things be equal, certainly preferable to one which assumes what is not actually given. There is good reason for this. We can argue namely that a trait which is certainly organic in the Fragment and is not contradicted by the data of the Episode was probably also organic in the latter. If we assume the presence of such a trait in the Episode at a point where it is possible, we operate with a feature which can be assigned a definite, historically attested, place in the organism of the story, which must therefore have more inherent probability than an alternative possibility that is without the same guarantee.

There still remains the question raised by the ambiguity of *treowe*. This, however, solves itself if we use, as above proposed, the situation given in the Fragment. Its resolution is, however, by no means a simple matter if we choose to abide by the assumption of litotes, but the discussion of this I have reserved for my second Appendix, to which the reader is referred.

To sum up: the most probable explanation of ll. 1071–72 *a* is that Hildeburh's situation was so tragic that she could not feel a spark of admiration for the heroic bearing of her brother's retainers, which in any other circumstances would certainly have filled her with justifiable pride. Not perhaps a very modern way of putting it on the part of the old poet, but would it be for that the less effective?

To proceed. It is not an unnatural consequence of adopting the litotes alternative that *unsynnum* in l. 1072 is very usually connected with a rather modern idea of innocence. We find that either innocence is attributed to Hildeburh (*e.g.* Chambers: "guiltless, she lost at the war," etc.) or *unsynnum* has been emended to *unsynngum* in order to make her dead relatives innocent. Here we must, however, be careful. It is hardly doubtful that the earlier meaning of *synn* is "feud, enmity," hence its conversion into "sin" is in all probability due to theological influence. Now, personally, I do not doubt that the author of *Beowulf* was a Christian according to his lights, but this does not amount to a proof that he transmogrified his vocabulary as a great deal of Anglo-Saxon vocabulary was in the course of time transmogrified by the learned. He will not have converted words to Christian meanings except where he was forced to do so by the necessity of expressing Christian ideas. For the main purposes of his narrative, however, he would not very often be under this necessity; and wherever such necessity is not present and there is a choice between the older meaning of a word and its later, Christian meaning, it will be safer to abide by the older meaning if it makes good sense. *Synn*, therefore, in *Beowulf* will only mean *culpa* or *peccatum* where these Christian ideas are likely to be present to the poet's mind; otherwise it means "feud," and *mutatis mutandis*, similar considerations hold good for its derivatives or compounds. Thus *synnig* applied once to Grendel (l. 1379) may mean "sinful," for the poet has obviously done his best to Christianize the conception of the monster, but in the one passage where the manuscript offers *unsynnigne* (l. 2089) this does not mean "sinless, innocent," but "harmless, unoffending." Beowulf is describing to Hygelac how Grendel tried to push him into his bag in Heorot. It is absurd to suppose that under these circumstances he would wish to insist on his innocence to his friend. No, Grendel, having satiated the first pangs of appetite on the body of the *slæpendne rinc* (l. 741), looks around him and sees Beowulf lying there, to all appearance an unresisting victim, harmlessly asleep[1], and hence seeks to bundle him without further ado into the sack.

Now it is of course possible that Christian notions of *culpa* or *peccatum* were teasing the poet's mind when he told the tale of Finn and Hengest; he *may* have been anxious to insist that Hildeburh was guiltless of her brother's blood, though in view of the passive rôle she plays in the tragedy, such insistence seems little called for; or he *may* have been anxious to settle the war-guilt and leave it on the proper shoulders. On the other hand it is possible that he was concerned about none of these things. Mr Chambers has shown very acutely that it does not follow even from the litotes alternative that Finn is to be regarded as a guilty person, but if not Finn, why anyone? We must at any rate admit that there is a possible alternative to the poet's being desirous to fix the guilt, namely, his not being desirous. For *unsynnum* is a hapax legomenon —we cannot say with certainty what it means, but only that its meaning must be derived from *syn*, *either* in the meaning "feud" or in the meaning "sin." We do not escape from this

---

[1] Clark Hall's "unoffending me" is consequently a better translation than Gering's "frei von Fehl." Is Grendel credited with a malign power of fascinating or hypnotizing his victims? This *might* be the meaning of the puzzling *swefeð ond sendeð* (l. 600), *i.e.* "lulls to sleep and despatches." It is noticeable that the victims make generally no resistance, cp. l. 122.

by emending to *unsynngum*, as is apparent from the above remarks on the only passage in *Beowulf* where this word really appears.

Can we find a meaning for *unsynnum* by starting from the meaning of *synn* as "feud, enmity"? About the form there is no doubt, because we can compare it with such an adverbial dat. plur. as *unwearnum*. Now as *unwearnum* from *wearn* means "without hindrance," so *unsynnum* can mean "without feud, *i.e.* in the absence of feud, although there was no feud."

Once more we arrive at two alternatives: *unsynnum* can mean either "guiltlessly" or "in the absence of feud." Can we estimate which is the more probable? I think so. Either we are told that "Hildeburh, guiltless, lost her dear ones" or that she "lost them although there was no feud at the time, sc. between the parties concerned." Now it is not certain that the poet would wish to insist on the innocence of Hildeburh, while it *is* certain that he wished to bring out the full horror of the tragedy which deprived her of her nearest relatives. To defend her against a hypothetical imputation of complicity in their death is, to say the least, a weak way of accomplishing this purpose. Contrariwise, to say that it took place in circumstances for which she could not be prepared, is a vigorous way. The pale figure of Hildeburh in the context drifts athwart the gloomy background of tragedy like a white dove in a charnel-house. To attribute to the poet anxiety for her blameless reputation is to credit him with an inartistic squeamishness. On the other hand, what could be more effective than to announce at once how on this dreadful occasion friend had raged against friend?

(1074 *bearnum ond broðrum;*)

Here again we have ambiguity, because it has been shown that the meaning may be "brother and child." The greater probability is, however, distinctly on the side of "brothers and children," for whether we regard these forms as plurals put for singulars, or as duals, in either case we have a merely occasional variation from general usage, whose presence here

could only be established by concurrent evidence. The sole
evidence of this sort is, however, firstly the negative fact that
a brother or brothers of Hnæf are not elsewhere mentioned,
which, considering the restricted nature of our sources of
information, cannot weigh heavily; and secondly the fact that
in l. 1115 the MS. suggests that Hildeburh had only one son.
This suggestion of the MS. is, however, as I shall try to show
later, not conclusive, and if I have reasoned correctly above
is contradicted by the *eaferum* in l. 1068.

> 1076   Nalles holinga   Hoces dohtor
>   meotod-sceaft bemearn,   syþðan morgen com,
>   ða heo under swegle   geseon meahte
>   morþor-bealo maga.

Chambers has shown satisfactorily that the fight in the
hall described in the Fragment is the *lind-plega* of l. 1073,
and this result will be borne out by further evidence adduced
below. He has further satisfactorily explained the apparent
discrepancy between *syþðan morgen com* and the five days of
fighting in the Fragment[1]. By these results of his I abide,
and note here the important indication thus established, that
hostilities broke out in the night-time.

> 1079 *b*   Þær he ær mæste heold
>   worolde wynne,

Chambers, who in his edition of *Beowulf* very properly
rejected the popular emendation of *he* to *heo*, pointed out that
this sentence contained a valuable indication by which to
localize the *lind-plega* of l. 1073. It was in and around the
mead-hall of Finn that his men fell. This is borne out by
a deeper comprehension of the phrase *worolde wynne*[2].

Wyn denotes the abstract idea of "delight." It is, therefore,
often rendered more concrete by expressing either the cause
of delight or the person or persons who feel it. The cause is

---

[1] Cp. *Introduction to Beowulf*, p. 260.

[2] Schücking seems to me to have missed the following point in his
discussion of this expression, see *Untersuchungen zur Bedeutungslehre der
Angelsächsischen Dichtersprache*, pp. 99 ff.

generally indicated by a dependent genitive as in *mægenes wyn*, the delight which arises from physical strength. But delight may be the result of a particular cause, as in the above example, or of general causes which need not be specified. This sort of general delight is indicated by the genitive of such words as *woruld, eorðe, lif*. Consequently *eorðan* and *lifes wyn* are synonyms of *worulde wyn*. Now delight in general may be the possession of any individual, of noble or peasant, of rich or poor man, but it is obvious that we associate it more particularly with favoured classes of individuals than less favoured. The general causes of delight we thus conceive as being more typically present in the case of a rich man than a poor man. The question therefore arises: Was there any position in life with which the general idea of delight was associated by the author of *Beowulf* more closely than with any other? The very interesting passage (ll. 1724*b*–57), in which Hrothgar enlarges on the ways of God to man, enables us to answer this question in the affirmative. There we read how God does to the man of noble birth, *i.e.*

> seleð him on eþle   eorþan wynne
> to healdanne   hleo-burh wera.

Before I make use of this parallel I must, however, deal with the translation of *eorðan wynne* indicated in the glossary to several of the Heyne editions[1], viz. "die liebliche Erde." If delight have a particular cause which in its turn is the effect of another cause, it may be a matter of indifference whether I speak of the delight which springs from something, or the something which causes delight. In this case the phrase which denotes "delight springing from a cause" may be equivalent in meaning to one which denotes the cause of delight. This is so, for instance, in the passage, *Beowulf* 2107:

> *Hwilum hilde-deor hearpan wynne, gomen-wudu grette.*

It is here a matter of indifference whether it be said "the warrior awoke the delight of the harp," or "he awoke the harp that causes delight"; since in this case the sound of the

[1] Not, however, in the last one (1918).

harp is both cause and effect. Hence the first phrase may stand for the second, and that it does so here, is proved by the parallel accusative *gomen-wudu*. In the same way it is a matter of indifference whether I say "God gave him the delight which springs from physical strength," or "He gave him the physical strength which brings delight." Hence *mægenes wynnum* in l. 1716 is correctly translated by "liebliche Heldenkraft," as the parallel *eafeðum* of the next line shows. But this only holds good where the delight indicated springs from a particular object. Where it is the effect of general causes which may combine in very various ways it does not hold good. Thus, evidently, "God gave him the world's delight" is not by any means the same thing as saying "God gave him the delightful world." Hence *eorðan wynne* cannot mean "die liebliche Erde." The person who so translated it first obviously overlooked the important distinction between delight as the product of general causes and as the product of a particular cause.

Granted the truth of what has been just said, we must translate ll. 1730–31 as follows: "God gives him on his land the world's delight, to hold the sheltering citadel of men (*i.e.* the castle in which men enjoy the protection of the *eorla hleo*)." Now l. 1731 is syntactically dependent on *seleð*[1] and therefore equivalent to a noun in the accusative; consequently it is parallel to, and in meaning an explanation of, *eorðan wynne* in the preceding line[2]. It is earthly bliss in a typical sense to be a ruler of men, according to this conception. The world's delight belongs in a special sense to the chieftain in his castle, ruling and protecting his retainers. We see, therefore, that the conception of worldly delight was associated for the poet with the person, and localized in the castle[3], of a chieftain. It is a natural conception for the man who dwells so lovingly

---

[1] Cp. *þonne him frea sylle to ongietanne godes bibod, Wunder der Schöpfung*, Grein-Wülker, iii, p. 153, l. 29; also *Beowulf*, l. 3055.

[2] On such "variation" of a noun by an infinitive phrase, see Klaeber, *Mod. Phil.* iii, 237 f.

[3] The same localization occurs in l. 28 of the "Seafarer" (*se ðe ah lifes wyn gebiden in burgum*).

on the social intercourse in Heorot and the rôle of the *beag-gyfa*, Hrothgar. From this it follows that the holder of *worulde wynne* in ll. 1079–80 can only be Finn, not his wife, and the place referred to, his *hleo-burg*.

An apparent objection to this conclusion is that a relative *þær*-clause usually follows its principal sentence. But this is a consequence of the general rule that the dependent sentence comes after the main statement in *Beowulf*, and this rule evidently admits of exceptions for the sake of emphasis, *i.e.* when the psychological importance of the dependent statement forces it into the consciousness of the speaker ahead of the main fact. The great regularity with which the *þær*-clause follows must not blind us as to the possibility of its preceding. It is an obvious result of the fact that psychologically the locality of an action only rarely attains the prominence necessary to force it to the front. But the death of Finn's retainers in their own *hleo-burg* is quite sufficient to explain the order here. It is the same tragic contrast as had already occupied the poet's mind in describing the doings at Heorot.

The fight referred to in what follows was consequently localized at Finn's burg. This is quite sufficient to identify it with the fight in the Fragment. For there are only two fights in the Episode, this one in which Hnæf falls, and the one at the end in which Finn falls. The intercalated fight in which, according to some, Hengest fell, is merely imaginary, as I hope the subsequent line of argument will show. Both fights took place in Finn's hall, but as in the second one the defenders were certainly the Frisians, it cannot possibly be the same as the fight in the Fragment, in which the defenders are just as certainly the Danes. The latter must consequently be identical with the first fight in the Episode. This result is of importance, for it shows that Hnæf and his men in this first fight were defending Finn's hall against Finn's men— a situation parallel to that of the Burgundians at the court of Etzel in the *Nibelungenlied*. But the only indications of this in the Episode are ll. 1086 and 1125 ff.

1080 *b*   wig ealle fornam
              Finnes þegnas,   nemne feaum anum,

This sentence deserves scrutiny in regard to the light it throws on Finn's losses and their bearing on the motives which led him to conclude a treaty with the Danes. It is necessary to note that it is only said that Finn lost nearly all his retainers, *i.e.* the greater part of his retinue (using this word with the sense of the German "Gefolgschaft"). Now Finn's retinue cannot be identified with the whole of his fighting forces, though it is possible that on the principle of *pars pro toto* it might stand for them. How much probability is there, however, attaching to this possibility? The members of Finn's retinue would doubtless be the officers and leaders of his army when it was assembled, but to say that an army lost the most of its officers is not at all the same thing as to say that it lost the most of its men. It by no means follows, therefore, that if Finn's army was engaged, the slaughter among Finn's thanes had reduced it to impotence, though it doubtless would be the occasion of a great reduction in its efficiency. Have we now any indication by which to measure this reduction, supposing it to have taken place? I think we have. The Fragment, which as already remarked describes the fight we are now speaking of, tells us that the Danish detachment engaged numbered sixty. Such a detachment might well put up a strong resistance even against an army, if, as they actually were, entrenched in a hall, especially under the conditions of ancient warfare; but even in those days sixty men were certainly not an army. It follows that if Hnæf came to Friesland on a warlike expedition, he must have been cut off from the mass of his forces; if, on the other hand, he came in time of peace (for which, as I have tried to show above, *unsynnum* in l. 1072 speaks), then the sixty formed his retinue. In either case he must have been facing fearful odds when fighting broke out in the hall, for even if the times were peaceful and the Frisian army consequently not on a war-footing, Finn at his own castle, as a mighty ruler, would have at his disposal a much larger contingent, which could furthermore be readily reinforced[1], than the stranger monarch. Under these circumstances the loss of even all his thanes would not mean that Finn was at the mercy of the small band that had followed Hnæf. The latter might be safe enough inside their fort, but they would still be in a foreign country, surrounded by foes, and doomed to destruction as soon as they emerged into the open.

> 1082   þæt he ne mehte   on þæm meðel-stede
>   wig Hengeste   wiht gefeohtan,

The cognate accusative and the personal dative (instead of the usual construction of *wið* and dative) in l. 1083 were for long a stumbling-block to the critics. No one, however, produced a generally acceptable emendation and when Klaeber, who had once[2] described the dative as scarcely possible here, discovered that this judgment went too far[3], little excuse was left for anyone to tamper with the line as it stands. If I am right in supposing, as I did above, that the employment of a comitative dative was once much more extensive than appears in the manuscripts, there can be little doubt that such a dative would be permissible with *feohtan*, for it is hardly possible to fight except in company with an opponent[4]; hence the hypothesis of the survival of an older construction would apply here as in the case of *eaferum* above.

Nor can it be said that there is any particular difficulty in making sense of the MS. reading. The verb *gefeohtan* certainly developed the meaning "win," as in the phrase *sige gefeohtan*, and there is therefore no *a priori* objection to some translation such as "he could not at all win the fight from Hengest." But the *a priori* view is apt to be misleading in historical judgments and it is better to regard it as a hint of the direction in which an explanation may be sought than an explanation in itself. The meaning of "win" for *gefeohtan* may not have

---

[1] Of Etzel and Kriemhilt in an analogous situation and after a terrible mowing down of their retainers, it is said "*daȝ lant daȝ was ir eigen; des mêrte sich ir schar.*" (*Der Nibelunge Not*, Sievers, 2089.)

[2] *Anglia*, xxviii, 444.   [3] *J.E.G. Phil.* xiv, 548.

[4] Cp. English "to fight with," German "mit einem streiten."

been developed so early as the date of *Beowulf*. On the other hand its development was evidently conditioned by the fact that *gefeohtan* was a perfective verb, which, in contrast with *feohtan* the continuous verb, meant "to fight to a finish," "to bring fighting to an end." There can be no doubt that *gefeohtan* would have the latter meaning at the earliest date.

Now the Fragment tells us that Hnæf's men defended the hall at Finn's burg for five days. It is even probable that the struggle lasted longer, for at the end of that time none of the defenders had fallen, and it cannot have come to a conclusion before Hnæf fell. This is a clear sign that Finn found it a very difficult matter to put a finis to the contest, and there would be nothing surprising if we were informed that after losing the most of his thanes he gave it up as a bad job. The language of the above passage certainly admits a meaning in harmony with this, viz. "so that he was not at all able to bring the fight with Hengest to an end." This does not, of course, contradict the conclusion we had already arrived at that the Danes were in a desperate position. It is not said that under any circumstances Finn would have been unable to finish with the Danes. On the contrary we have the limitation duly denoted: *on þæm meðel-stede*, at that meeting-place, *i.e. þær he ær mæste heold worolde wynne*. This plainly reminds us of the entrenched situation of the Danes in the hall, which is guaranteed by the Fragment. Of course a besieged garrison may be in a hopeless fix and yet able to beat off the attacks of the besiegers. All that is told us here is that Finn despaired of reducing the garrison by direct attack. It is not implied that he had no other means of dealing with them. The upshot then is that the first fight in Finn's burg was a draw, a stale-mate. It did not end decisively for either party, but was broken off, left "unentschieden."[1]

---

[1] Ayres, without discussing the wording of our passage, had already seen that this was contained in the situation (see *Journal of English and Germantc Philology*, XVI, 287).

1084   ne þa wea-lafe   wige forþringan
       þeodnes ðegne;

Here we have two difficult words, the extremely rare *forþringan*, and *wea-lafe*. I will deal with the verb first.

To construct a meaning for *forþringan* we have only such indications as are given by the context and its own formative elements. The latter, however, are ambiguous, since the prefix *for* has many meanings and *þringan* may be either transitive or intransitive. The context shows at any rate that the compound is transitive. The situation suggests that it is a question of keeping something from an opponent, or wresting something from him. Since it is usual to give *wea-lafe* a personal reference (on which see below, p. 43 f.) it is generally assumed that *forþringan* means "protect." I have, however, grave doubts whether this meaning can be established by the comparison with *forstandan*[1], which apart from the situation is its strongest support. The latter word could only be a real parallel if *forþringan* were formed from the intransitive verb. Now it would certainly be legitimate to judge the possible meaning of a compound of intransitive *þringan* with *for* by appealing to a similar compound formed from a word of allied meaning, but as regards this point I have the following considerations to offer. Both *þringan* and *standan* belong to the class of primary verbs of motion, denoting a change of situation[2]. This class shows two subdivisions, containing verbs denoting (*a*) continuous motion, like *cuman, gan*, (*b*) perfective motion, like *standan*, "to cease moving in an upright posture, come to a stand." The first group is more numerous than the second, containing such common words as *bugan, cuman, faran, gan, hweorfan, iernan, ridan*, while the second has only *licgan, sittan, standan*. To the first group we may also add the secondary formations *feran* and *hwierfan, cierran*, so far as they are intransitive, and the primary verb *sceotan* so far as it also is intransitive. All, or the most of these words[3] form *for*-compounds, with

---

[1] Cp. *Sprachschatz*[2], *s.v.*   [2] Cp. Postscript, p. 169.
[3] Some are doubtful, *e.g. foriernan, forsceotan*, neither of which is booked by Sweet although he gives *fore-iernend* and *fore-sceotan*.

which, however, we are obviously only concerned in so far as the resultant compound is transitive.

If we compare the transitive *for*-compounds of both groups the following facts are noticeable.

The only type of meaning which is common to both groups is the privative one of avoidance, neglect and their nuances, represented *e.g.* by *forbugan, forcierran, forgan, forsittan*. This is natural, because in the first group the privative notion might result from the idea of passing by, or removing from, and in the second from that of keeping, holding one's distance. On the other hand it cannot be accidental that certain types of meaning are peculiar to *one* group. Thus, destruction (*forfaran, forcuman*), and surpassing, conquering (*forcuman*) only appear among the verbs of the first group—obstruction (*forstandan* and *forsittan*), protection (*forstandan, forlicgan*) only among the verbs of the second group. Parallel to the last-mentioned circumstance runs the fact that the construction of accusative plus dative is also restricted to the second group. The only (doubtful!) exception to this that I can find is a sentence in the Chronicle (*a.* 897): *forforon him þone muðan foran on utermere*. It may be that this points to the possibility of a verb of the continuous group developing the meaning of obstruction, but the matter is doubtful on account of the *foran*. We must compare two analogous instances of *forridan* with a personal object also in the Chronicle, and also combined with *foran*, for which reason Sweet in the *Student's Dictionary* quite correctly quotes the compound *foran forridan*. It looks as if the prefix *for* in these words merely made the verb transitive, or at most gave it a perfective sense (rode, sailed, up to). The idea of cutting off (obstruction) is then given by the addition of *foran*, "from in front." It is rather notable that *forstandan*. both in the sense of obstruction and protection, likewise occurs in conjunction with *foran(e)*; but this circumstance is negligible here since these meanings are well attested both in poetry and prose without any such assistance.

If together with the above we take into consideration that

intransitive *þringan* belongs to the first of the above groups, and that its being compounded at all with *for* is not unambiguously attested, I think it must appear very doubtful whether we are at liberty to compare our *forþringan* with *forstandan*. In these circumstances there is hardly anything left but to attempt an explanation on the hypothesis that we have here a compound formed with transitive *þringan*. When we do this the well attested *oþþringan* offers itself, with a suitable meaning and a suitable construction. This is almost certainly formed from the transitive verb, since combination with *oþ* does not generally make transitive compounds from intransitive simple verbs. The meaning is therefore correctly given by Sweet as "force away from one, deprive." Since the prefixes *for* and *oþ* often agree in function, there can be little objection to regarding *forþringan* and *oþþringan* as synonyms. Compare Appendix N, pp. 166 ff.

Finally, as having a bearing on the question whether *forþringan* is derivable from the transitive or intransitive verb, it may be as well to point out that compounds of *for* with primary intransitive verbs of motion are far more characteristic of prose than poetry. The *Sprachschatz* only records *forbugan* (two occurrences), *forcuman*, *forgangan* (once), *forlicgan* (twice), *forsittan* (twice as transitive, twice intransitive), *forstandan*, *forhwyrfan*. Of these possibly *forgangan* is to be rejected (= præire, Psalm lxxxviii. 13): it is doubtful whether the true *for*-compounds of this class ever had originally the meaning of precedence, and its nuances (*e.g.* prevention, anticipation); this only occurs in translations from Latin, and here *for*- alternates with *fore*-. Sweet ignores such meanings of *forgan*, etc. in his *Student's Dictionary*[1]. Further, since *forhwyrfan* only occurs with the meaning "pervertere, transformare," it is doubtful whether it represents the intransitive simple verb. More likely it comes from the transitive.

Wea-laf I hold to be ambiguous. It may denote either

---

[1] Cp. also R. Dittes in *Anglia*, Beiblatt XXII, 129 ff. for occasional discussion of such words.

"something *or* somebody that survives disaster." This is not generally recognized, because the only other two instances of *wea-laf*, one in poetry[1] and one in prose[2], both mean "survivors." But this is not decisive, as, I think, the following argumentation will show. The instances of *laf* as simplex in the *Sprachschatz* (new ed.) fall into two main classes, those in which it is accompanied by a genitive denoting who or what left the *laf*, and those in which this is not the case. The first of these classes shows that the *laf* is conceived in two ways: as something which outlasts the destructive action of an agent (*e.g. wæpna laf, fyres laf*—I say *agent* advisedly, not instrument, because as cases like *ic eom wraðra fyres ond feole laf* prove, the instrument was personified[3]); and as something which outlived its owner (*e.g. Eanmundes, gomelra laf*). From this it may be seen that the *laf* is associated with a personal or at least personified origin, and is originally a *thing*, which only comes by personification to denote living beings. The instances of the simplex *laf* in the second main class all show by some indication or other their relation to either the agent or the owner group of the first main class. Thus, apart from the idiom *to lafe*, when it belongs to the owner group it has the conventional epithet *eald* or *gamol*; belonging to the agent group it has the epithet *earm* or a genitive of the person or thing that survives (in one instance both of these signs, *Daniel* l. 80).

The compounds of *la* likewise fall into two classes, according as the first element denotes a destructive agent or has an adjectival force denoting the class of object which is so called. Thus the first group contains *yð-laf* (that which survives the attack of the breakers = shore), *sæ-laf* (what is tossed up by the sea), and *wea-laf* (what survives disaster). The second group has *ende-laf* (last survival), *here-laf* (remainder of an army), *yrfe-laf* (relic, not of an inheritance, but which belongs to an inheritance), *eormen-laf* (great relic),

---

[1] *Metra*, I, 22.   [2] *Wulfstan*, 133, 13.
[3] Does this personification explain the difference between *feole laf* and the Latin *reliquiae limae*, cp. Cook, *Amer. Journ. of Phil.* VI, 479?

perhaps also *incge-laf* (precious relic? cp. below, p. 72 f.). *Ege-laf* must be left aside as too uncertain[1]; it would, of course, belong to the first group of compounds.

By hypothesis all of these could refer either to things or by personification to persons, with the single exception of *here-laf* whose attributive first element limits it to a personal reference. Since, however, none of the *laf*-compounds occurs often, it is not surprising that *yrfe-laf* is the only one which shows instances of the double reference. On the other hand, if we leave out the exceptional *here-laf* and the uncertain *ege-laf* (and *incge-laf*) as well as the present doubtful instance of *wea-laf*, and then count the occurrences, we get the result that in poetry (following the *Sprachschatz*) there are five instances of *laf*-compounds referring to things and five referring to persons[2]. That is just the result we should expect to find, as long as we are dealing with compounds *not* of a type which is limited by the first member to a single reference. It may consequently be tested from this point of view. We saw above that the meanings of *laf* belong to the two divisions I called the agent and the owner groups. The first of these falls into three sub-groups, which may be called the tool sub-group (*e.g. hamera laf*), the weapon sub-group (*e.g. dareða laf*), and the vicissitude sub-group (*e.g. wætra, lago-siða laf*). In the compounds only the second main, *i.e.* owner group, and the third, *i.e.* vicissitude, *sub-group* of the first main group are represented. As the tool sub-group, which by nature can only denote things, and the weapon sub-group, which by nature can only denote living beings, are not represented, it follows that all the attested compounds (aside from the before mentioned *here-laf*) could by nature be used of either things or persons. In any single occurrence of such a compound there is therefore an equal chance of its referring to a person or a thing, and the proportion 5 to 5 in all the occurrences counted conforms closely to this. When we consider further that the

---

[1] MS. *ece lafe*, *Exodus*, 370.

[2] *sæ-lafe* (*Exodus*, 584) is, however, really ambiguous. It may well be acc. sing. and in that case has an impersonal reference.

relative paucity of these compounds shows that none of them is likely to have been fixed by usage with a conventional reference to one of the possible alternatives, and that the only one of them which occurs more than twice, namely *yrfe-laf*, has four equally divided instances, it seems highly probable that my assertion about *wea-laf* being ambiguous is well founded.

I proceed, therefore, to enquire whether we have so far any indication in the text to enable us to decide what is the reference of the word. Now as we have just learnt that Finn had no prospect of finishing the fight with Hengest, a statement that he could not wrest something from the latter by fighting (*wige*) must be one of two things, either mere tautology or an indication of his intention. We can with probability take it as the latter, and draw the conclusion that Finn wanted the *wea-laf* in his own possession. In the given circumstances there is of course a possibility that what Finn wanted to win from Hengest was *either* persons *or* things, but the probability that it was *one* of the two is quite a different matter. Asking, however, what test of probability we can apply, we can give the following answer. Since we must assume that the story is an organic whole, we cannot reasonably introduce any unknown feature into it which is not guaranteed by the features that are known. That is to say, no merely possible feature should be introduced unless its existence is rendered *probable* by others which are certainly there. The possibilities of Finn's wanting to wrest certain persons from Hengest's power are, of course, very various, but they can all be eliminated except in so far as they are not merely suggested but rendered probable by things which belong definitely to the story as it is presented to us.

There are, so far as I see, nothing more than hints that the *wea-laf* might be persons. These are two in number and I will take them in order.

The first is that since Finn has been attacking unsuccessfully he may have lost prisoners whom he is anxious to rescue. The description of the fight in the Fragment does not, however, suggest that the Danes were making prisoners: it too much resembles the fight at Etzel's court, where prisoners certainly were not made by the Burgundians[1]. Furthermore, a small garrison defending a hall is not likely to be keen on making prisoners. They would unduly complicate the task of defence against a greatly superior force. And as the struggle in the hall turned on vengeance it was surely a bitter one.

The second hint is that the Danes are later taken by Finn into his service. They were obviously doughty fighting men, and as a judge of such matters, Finn may, even while the fight was in progress, or possibly earlier, have formed a desire to become lord of their allegiance. Furthermore, as I hope to be successful in showing, the Danes actually *are* separated from Hengest at a subsequent stage. This striking agreement, however, though it confirms the possibility of the *wea-laf* being survivors on the Danish side, so far as l. 1084 is concerned, has to be harmonized with other references, and the discussion of these I reserve for the present.

It need hardly be pointed out that when we decided above that the fight was a drawn one we eliminated the possibility that *wea-lafe* might refer to Finn's own warriors outside the hall. We saw that although he despairs of breaking down the resistance of the Danes he had no reason to be afraid of them if they should come out of their fortress. So long as he does not attack, therefore, he need not fear any further losses. The situation consequently forbids both that *wea-lafe* should refer to Finn's forces and that *forþringan* should have the meaning "protect," which has above been rejected on linguistic grounds.

1085 b   ac hig him geþingo budon,

With this half-line we approach that "tangle of 'thems' and 'theys'" of which Chambers[2] feelingly says: "Unfortunately, owing to the confusion of pronouns, we soon lose

---

[1] On the contrary, they throw both dead and wounded out of the hall (*Nibelungenlied*, Bartsch, 2013, 2014).

[2] *Introduction*, p. 250.

our way amidst the clauses of this treaty." Under these circumstances I might well exclaim "terrent vestigia!" but, since I believe that here as elsewhere it is possible to estimate the relative probability of the alternatives resulting from ambiguity, I take courage to proceed. Of course, in the given situation either side might have sufficient motives for offering to treat: Hengest because he is beleaguered with his small band in a foreign land; Finn because he has lost hope of reducing the obstinate garrison in the hall to subjection by fighting. The *hig* above might therefore *a priori* refer to either. But the poet certainly had only one of these alternatives in his mind, and the problem is to find indications to show which is more probable to have been present to him. I believe that the small word *ac* can be made to throw light on this problem.

Since *ac* is generally to be translated by "but," the negative sentence before it in *Beowulf* may appear to the modern reader to have a concessive force, as when we say "She is not beautiful, but charming." The temptation here to see such a concession is heightened by the fact that the subject of the following affirmative sentence is of a different number, and therefore appears to be different from the subject of the negative sentence. The modern reader consequently grasps instinctively at some such sense for the passage as this, "Finn was able to fight no longer, but they (viz. his opponents) offered terms." I admit that this is not contradicted by the situation, but I believe it can be shown that the negative sentence before *ac* in *Beowulf never* has a concessive force. The proof of this is too long to insert here, consequently I have reserved it for an Appendix[1].

The two sentences between which *ac* stands always form a whole which I call below by the name of "antithetic expansion." Underlying such a whole there is always a choice between a pair of alternative propositions, one of which must be negatived if the other is affirmed. In the situation given at this moment there are two pairs of such alternative pro-

---

[1] See Appendix III below, pp. 148 ff..

positions, either of which might naturally have presented itself to the mind of the poet. The one pair would be "Either Finn or the Danes offered a treaty"; the other would be "Either Finn fought on, or he offered a treaty." The first pair would have entailed the assertion that "one side did not offer a treaty, but the other did," and this is plainly not contained in the context. Remains the second pair. This would involve the statement (put in its simplest form), "Finn did not fight on, but he offered a treaty." This is obviously so close to the text that it can be accepted as its meaning, if it can be shown that in such a statement the number of the subject can vary from one sentence to another. There is no difficulty about this. Such variation is not unknown in the language of the epic and was obviously permissible when speaking of a person who is regarded not only as an individual but also as the representative of a group. There are further examples in the Episode alone, as we shall presently note, cp. also ll. 796–7[1]. Now Finn is here plainly thought of as the representative of the Frisian party. Furthermore, in ll. 1082–85 the poet is obviously concerned with presenting to us motives which Finn had for action, and he is not consequently likely to have mixed up with these an act which came from the other side.

However there is still a difficulty outstanding. I have tried to show by linguistic criteria what is the probably correct translation of ll. 1079 a–86 b, and I hope to have been successful, so far as such criteria admit, in establishing the sense of the passage. But even assuming my success in this respect, my translation has still, methodically speaking, only hypothetical value, until it can be shown to harmonize with as much knowledge of any sort as we can bring to bear on the matter in hand. Having argued from the language of the text that Finn found himself in a certain situation which was the reason for his offering terms to his opponents, I must therefore show that such action on his part does not con-

[1] Cp. also Sievers (*PBB.* xxix, 570) on the vagueness attaching to the expression of "summative" and collective ideas.

tradict what we know to hold good of human motives in general. I have argued, now, that the text shows Finn's reasons for negotiation to have been twofold, viz. (1) his inability in consequence of an unsuccessful attack to make any further assault with prospects of success, (2) his desire to obtain in another way what he despaired of obtaining by fighting. But Finn, I have further argued, though so far defeated is by no means hopeless. His foes are shut in and cannot escape. Under these circumstances the failure of an assault by no means necessarily entails an immediate offer of terms. We must therefore allow the possibility (which as we have seen is actually implicit in the text) of his having had two alternatives before him, viz. the immediate opening of negotiations or a continuance of hostilities by different tactics, and the question arises, Why did he reject the latter? I shall return to this point later, for the present it will suffice to call to mind that siege tactics as we understand them nowadays were then among the Germanic tribes in a very undeveloped state. Their adoption would likely have meant for Finn either firing his hall or enforcing a hunger blockade. Now it is noticeable that in the *Nibelungenlied* the Burgundians when penned in Etzel's hall obviously regard themselves as the victims of undue cruelty, and furthermore that the stringent measures on which Kriemhild insists are applied unwillingly by the Huns. It is only because Etzel *must* exact atonement for his son and lost friends that he refuses the offered treaty, and it is not he, but Kriemhild, in the rôle which she derives from the Sigfrid Saga, who gives the order to fire the hall and roast brave men who cannot be overcome in fair fight. It cannot be doubtful from this what the general sentiment as regards such things was. Now Hnæf is dead, Finn *has* exacted atonement—and a nod is as good as a wink to a blind horse!

Furthermore that in circumstances such as we are studying it was really not unusual for the leader of the attacking force to have recourse to negotiation instead of immediately applying the slower process of a hunger blockade, is suggested by an interesting historical parallel to be found in Gregory of Tours' *Historia Francorum* (Book 3, cap. xiv). Munderic rebelled against the Frankish monarch Theuderic, and when the latter sent an army against him took refuge in Victoriacum, which the army proceeded to invest. The attack was kept up for seven days without result.

These things were told the king, and Gregory goes on, "At ille misit quendam de suis, Aregisilum nomine, dixitque ei: Vides, inquit, quod praevaleat hic perfidus in contumacia sua. Vade, et redde ei sacramentum ut securus egrediatur." Of course Theuderic, being a Merovingian, had, as he at once explains to his envoy, a traitorous design. It proves successful, for Munderic, despite his successful resistance and a not unnatural suspicion of disloyal intent, is so impressed by the envoy's representations regarding the fate that will overtake him through starvation, that he gives in and accepts the proffered oath. Here then we have the following resemblances with the situation in the Finn Saga: (1) attacks prolonged for some time by a superior besieging party, which have no success; (2) recognition by the besiegers that the defenders cannot be defeated in fair fight; (3) recognition by both parties that the defenders are nevertheless in a hopeless position; (4) offer to treat made by the attackers. There is the important difference that in the Saga the offer is loyally intended, while in the historical instance this is not so. In the latter case, however, there would have been no use in making it if there had not been a presumption that it could be made without traitorous intent. It must therefore have been regarded as a natural thing to do in such circumstances, and it was not so much the offer in itself as Munderic's knowledge of Theuderic's character, which made him hesitate to accept it.

If my argument that it was considered a natural thing to make an *honest* offer to treat to a garrison which had put up a successful fight against superior force, is correct, this could only be based on a sporting instinct of fair play which forbad the use of the extremest measures (burning or hungering out)

4–2

against plucky fighters. It does not speak against this that the combination of a *traitorous* invitation with a house-burning was a common one in Teutonic poetry[1]. On the contrary, this plainly represents the feeling that only traitors would be likely to adopt such savage means of attaining their ends. Such measures were, however, obviously regarded as very effective, if not irresistible; and since the threat of their being used would always be in the background, this would balance the disadvantage under which honest besiegers would labour as negotiators in having to acknowledge that they recognized their inability to accomplish anything by fighting.

> 1086 þæt hie him oðer flet   eal gerymdon,
>   healle ond heah-setl,

The verb *geryman* means literally "to make room" and is generally construed with a dative of the person for whom, and an accusative either of the direction, or the space, in which room is made; hence it denotes clearing or throwing open a way, place or building. There can be consequently no doubt that the passage above means "that they should throw open to them the whole of another dwelling, a hall with its throne." Clear as the text is, there are, however, considerable ambiguities in its implications. To whom, we must ask again, does *hie* refer, to Finn's party or Hengest's? Does *oðer* mean a second hall in addition to, or one in place of, the one *not* already explicitly mentioned? Finally, is the clearing of the hall only to be understood as a sharing of it between the two parties or as a complete abandonment of its possession by one party to the other? Before we deal with these ambiguities it will be helpful to point out as a set-off to them, that the mention of "another flat" is a clear proof that a first hall was involved in the poet's conception of the situation which led up to the negotiations. If a second hall is to be thrown open either in addition to, or in place of, a first hall, as part of a treaty, that can only mean that occupation of the latter was at stake in the preceding quarrel.

---

[1] Cp. Neckel, *Beiträge zur Eddaforschung*, 1908, p. 178.

Starting from this we may by elimination be able to decide among the various thinkable hypotheses as to the reference of *hie* and the alternative implications of *oðer*.

(1) If we suppose that the Danes were to make the Frisians free of a second additional hall, this would involve the assumption that the Frisians had already taken a first hall from the Danes in the fight.

(2) If we suppose that the Danes were to clear another hall as substitute for the first, this involves the assumption that they had successfully preserved possession of the first and were to keep it at the expense of a *quid pro quo* in kind.

(3) If we suppose that the Frisians were to clear a second additional hall, this would presuppose that they were to give up their claim to the one for which they had fought.

(4) If we suppose that the Frisians were to clear another hall as substitute, this would involve the assumption that the Danes had successfully defended the first, but were to abandon it in exchange for access to the second.

We have already seen how the fighting had been on the most probable hypothesis "in and around Finn's mead-hall" (Chambers), *þær he ær mæste heold worolde wynne*; how further, since this is also the situation described in the Fragment, it is beyond all else probable that the Danes were the occupants and successful defenders of the hall, and how in consequence Finn had decided to offer terms. It follows, therefore, that these terms must reflect motives that can be attributed fairly to Finn, and that we can estimate the relative probability of the four alternatives just stated above from this standpoint. Now if Finn has failed to turn the Danes out of his hall by fighting he will naturally be inclined to accomplish this end, if possible, through the negotiations on which he has decided to enter. On the other hand, the Danes whose safety depends on their entrenched position in the hall will hardly be likely to consent to abandon that position for nothing. Finn would not display much tact as a negotiator if he were to propose to a garrison, flushed by a successful defence of their fortress, that they should simply abandon it.

He might, however, hope that they should show some willingness to do this, if offered in exchange a place which would possess similar tactical possibilities, and be a fair guarantee of their security so long as they held it.

Of the above alternatives it is clear by inspection that only the fourth is in harmony with any motives which can be attributed to Finn as opener of the negotiations. It would in the situation, as we have reconstructed it, be quite natural for him to propose that the Danes should restore his hall, receiving in exchange one of similar dignity, *i.e.* a hall with a throne. Finn as a powerful king has doubtless several such at his disposal, but if in the circumstances it is politic for him to grant the Danes leave to occupy *one* of them, he will naturally be averse to that one being his residence. At this point it furthermore becomes clear that there can hardly be a question of sharing a hall between the two parties. If the Danes are to be given a guarantee of security equal to that they already possess in the hall they have successfully defended, they must be given complete possession of the new hall. The emphatic *eal* (it bears the third alliterative stave!) of l. 1086, therefore, receives additional significance. Its function is doubtless to convey that it is a question of handing over another *flet*, not of merely allowing the Danes to come in as guests. Here the contrast between *eal geryman* and the *innanweard geryman* of ll. 1975–76 assumes importance. In the latter passage Hygelac's *flet* is being prepared for the celebration of Beowulf's homecoming: *eal* plainly makes the verbal idea inclusive and expresses a total clearance; *innanweard* obviously limits the clearance to the interior. In the first case the whole space in question is cleared, in the second, room is made for an additional person or persons inside the hall. *Eal geryman* consequently expresses the idea of handing over, giving possession of; *innanweard geryman* of sharing occupation.

1087 b   þæt hie healfre geweald
         wið Eotena bearn   agan moston,

The literal meaning is again quite clear[1]: "that they should be allowed to have power of the half with the son (or sons) of the Eotens," but the reference of both *hie* and *healfre* calls for investigation.

The latter word cannot refer, as often taken to do, to *healle* immediately preceding, since, as shown above, the hall is to be given over completely to the Danes. The only other alternative is to connect it with *wea-lafe* in l. 1084. As we have already decided that the *wea-laf* is intimately associated with Finn's motives in offering a treaty, there can be nothing surprising in finding a mention of it in one of the clauses. Still leaving a final decision as to the exact nature of this *wea-laf* for further consideration, we know it to be for the present in Hengest's power; consequently, those who are to be permitted power over one half of it are probably the Frisians (rather than *vice versa*) and the *Eotena* refers, in harmony with our interpretation of l. 1072 *a*, once more to the Danes.

It is, of course, not quite satisfactory that *healfre* should be made to agree with a word occurring three lines back, but various considerations speak strongly for such a connection. Firstly, if we emend to *healfne* we gain nothing, for we have in this case, either, to understand, as the enlargement of *geweald*: *þæs flettes* or *þære wea-lafe*, thus arriving at the same alternatives as above; or, we have to take *geweald* absolutely and so introduce some condition dealing with a division of sovereignty between the parties, which is contradicted by the subsequent relations between Finn and the Danes, who acknowledge him as their *beag-gyfa*. Secondly, since the terms of the treaty must undoubtedly reflect in the poet's mind the motives of Finn, the *wea-laf* which the latter has been trying to wrest from Hengest must loom largely in his (the poet's) consciousness, and he may therefore have easily referred to it in a way, not obviously vague to him, but so to a modern

[1] Apart, of course, from the ambiguous form of *bearn* (singular or plural) which for the present can be neglected.

reader: all the more so because he is giving a précis of the tale recited by Hrothgar's scop and consequently, as before noted, striving for the utmost concision of expression. It is besides possible, as will appear hereafter, that what immediately follows was sufficient to make the reference of *healfre* clear to his auditors.

```
1089   ond æt feoh-gyftum      Folcwaldan sunu
       dogra gehwylce      Dene weorþode,
       Hengestes heap       hringum wenede,
       efne swa swiðe      sinc-gestreonum
       fættan goldes,       swa he Fresena cyn
       on beor-sele    byldan wolde.
```

This is not a new clause in the treaty, as is shown by its not being introduced by *þæt*—it therefore forms part of a clause along with the preceding condition referring to the distribution of *geweald*. It is noticeable now that the first clause mentioned as part of the treaty offered to be made, implies a concession and counter-concession, since, according to this, the Danes are to give up one hall and receive another for it. Hence we can infer that the two portions of the second clause are similarly balanced. Finn offers to treat the Danes at the sharing of treasure on equal terms with his own men in consideration of their making over to him the disposal of a half of the *wea-laf*. The Danes being on the same footing with the Frisians as regards the distribution of rewards by the king of the latter, implies of course that they are to become the retainers of Finn, yet since by the first clause they are to possess a hall and throne of their own, there must be something exceptional in the position offered to them. Certainly they are not to become part of his household.

```
1095   Ða hie getruwedon      on twa healfa
       fæste frioðu-wære;
```

From these lines it is evident that the Danes are conceived as accepting the terms offered by Finn without bargaining or at any rate in the form in which they have just been stated.

This throws by implication important light on the motives of both sides.

As regards the Danes, they are obviously abandoning their obligation to avenge their slaughtered lord, a duty which, as is shown by the sequel, could not be considered as discharged as long as Finn was alive, and further they are entering into Finn's service. There is only one explanation of this, that given in l. 1103, *þa him swa geþearfod wæs*, i.e. "der Not gehorchend, nicht dem eignen Trieb." This requires to be urged against Chambers' learned and ingenious attempt to prove that Finn was respectable and Hengest generous[1]. I quite believe in Finn's respectability according to the standard of his times, but I have strong doubts about the generosity of a man who acts under the pressure of necessity. There is no doubt, then, that the poet's conception is that the Danes, in spite of their hitherto successful resistance, were in a hopeless position. This bears out the argumentation by which I sought to prove above that Finn's position is by no means so helpless as it is often assumed to be. The situation is obviously analogous to that in the *Nibelungenlied* where the Burgundians likewise do prodigious slaughter among Etzel's men but know from the very beginning that they have no prospect of escape. Hengest accepts the inevitable, which is submission, in a situation in which he can see no chance of attaining the one end which would justify resistance to the last gasp, namely, the slaying of Finn, for Finn's person is in this struggle plainly as far beyond the reach of the Danes as Etzel's is beyond that of the Burgundians. Our distant forefathers may be credited with sufficient subtlety to enable them to distinguish between the duty of revenge and the duty to commit suicide, and the failure of the poet to express any distaste at Hengest's action, though only an argument *ex silentio*, is probably, in view of l. 1103, an indication that it could be regarded at any rate as excusable.

I do not think we need argue from the story in the Anglo-Saxon *Chronicle*[2] that it was held to be the *duty* of warriors

---

[1] Cp. *Introduction to Beowulf*, pp. 276 ff. and especially p. 279.
[2] Cp. Lawrence, *Pub. Mod. Lang. Soc. of America*, xxx, 405.

in the same circumstances as Hengest to immolate themselves on the altar of loyalty. Doubtless such conduct would be much admired, but there are always, and probably were even then, upholders of the "falsehood of extremes." The bearing of Cynewulf's thanes might be likened to the Charge of the Light Brigade—"c'est magnifique mais ce n'est pas la guerre."[1] And even the "Die-Hards" of those days would probably admit that Hengest was justified, if by nothing else, at least by the result. On the other hand, Hengest would certainly have deserved reprobation, if the advantage *had* been on his side and he had in spite of that come to terms. For, it must be noted, when Hnæf falls there has been sufficient bloodshed to represent a full atonement by the Danes, but—"der Fluch der bösen Tat, dass sie fortzeugend immer Böses muss gebären!"—there cannot now be sufficient bloodshed from a Danish point of view until Finn falls.

When Chambers[2] urges that "the death of Finn's son is a set off for the death of Hnæf" he is reducing the hypothesis of Finn's impotence *ad absurdum*, for he is implicitly arguing that the Danes could regard the slaying of Finn's son as a satisfactory substitute for slaying Finn himself, the *bana* of their lord. If they could, why all the subsequent pother, which obviously arises because from a Danish point of view full atonement has not been exacted by them?—The final tragedy springs of course from the Danes giving a promise they *could* not keep, but the only justification of their doing so acceptable to those times, was, as explained in l. 1103, their being under a compulsion which gave them no choice except between a useless sacrifice of their lives and submission.

Regarding Finn's motives in which there still remains the problem adumbrated above—it now becomes plain that Finn knew what he was about, if and when he rejected siege tactics as an alternative to offering a treaty; for he must have been certain that that would happen, which did happen, namely, that the Danes would accept his offer as the only escape from

---

[1] Similarly Ayres, *Journal of English and Germanic Philology*, xvi, 288.
[2] *Introduction*, p. 285.

virtual suicide. Finn can afford to be generous in the way
that, as Chambers well demonstrated in his investigation of
the ethics of the blood-feud, generosity was not infrequently
shown; for, since Hnæf is dead, the sons of Finn have been
fully avenged. Unlike Hildeburh, he may in these circumstances have been very well able to appreciate the valour of
Hnæf's retainers and even to wish that the allegiance of such
brave and efficient fighters should be transferred to himself,
especially since this transference would naturally involve his
obtaining possession of that *wea-laf* which was still in their
hands and the object of his cupidity. Besides this, as the
thoroughly respectable prince, whom Chambers has shown
him to be, Finn would naturally wish to establish his right to
the *wea-laf* by honourable means. According to the con-
ventions of the times there would hardly be more than two
ways of doing this, namely by fighting or agreement. Fighting
he has already tried and rejected as impracticable, consequently there only remains for an honourable man the path
of negotiation. In treading it Finn accepts risks, for he must
understand perfectly well that while the blood account may
be closed for him by the death of Hnæf, on the other hand it
still gapes open for the Danes. Unless he was truly stupid
he must have had measures in his eye to obviate the eventuality
of the Danes being swept away by the passion for revenge
still unsatisfied. There is no mention of such precautions on
his part in the poet's statement of the terms offered to the
Danes, but as we shall soon see, Finn was prepared.

> 1096 *b*   Fin Hengeste
>   elne unflitme   aðum benemde,

It is practically certain inference from l. 1095 that the
treaty was ratified by the swearing of oaths on both sides.
Why then, we must ask, does the poet delay his narrative
by singling out Finn's oath-taking for detailed mention? In
his précis of the tale told by Hrothgar's scop he would
naturally strive to avoid superfluous details. Whence comes it
then that, while Hengest's rôle as an oath-taker is passed

over in silence, he considered it necessary to devote as much attention to the formulae by which Finn confirmed, as to those in which he offered, the treaty? As a preliminary to answering this question I will consider the language of the text which is not without its difficulties. The verb *benemnan* can, in its literal sense, hardly have another meaning than "to give a name to, mention explicitly, specify"; *aðum benemnan* is therefore "to specify by oaths," or where the oaths are sworn in confirmation of what has already been arranged, "to confirm what is specified in the content of the oaths."

On the basis of a reasoning, which I will explain later when discussing the *unhlitme* of l. 1129, I consider *elne unflitme* to mean "freely and frankly in accordance with agreement." I translate therefore: "Finn swore to Hengest freely and frankly, in accordance with the previous arrangements, specific oaths to the effect, that etc."

Now an oath sworn in ratification of a treaty might be a general formula binding the swearer to faithful observance of the whole, or it might be a series of such formulae confirming the provisions severally and in detail. It is plain from the above and what follows that Finn did not use a general formula, and the question therefore arises, Did he swear to the clauses of the treaty severally, and that alone; or did he make promises over and above what was contained in the treaty? Since the oaths attributed to him do not correspond exactly to the terms mentioned in ll. 1086–94, the first presumption would be in favour of the latter alternative, which would give a simple explanation why the poet emphasized Finn's part in the oath-taking, namely, because Finn showed his generosity by swearing more than circumstances required of him. If, however, we put side by side in cold blood the two hypotheses, (1) that Finn confirmed the provisions of the treaty by oaths; and (2) that he confirmed a great deal more, I think it will be admitted that the first has inherently a great deal more probability than the second. We could, indeed, only accept the second if we had concurrent evidence that the poet wished to represent Finn as somewhat extravagantly generous, even at the risk of showing him to be an improvident guardian of his own and his party's interests; whereas, while a certain frank readiness to pledge his kingly honour would be to Finn's credit, that would only hold good within reasonable limits, which would be rather exceeded if he showed eagerness to pledge himself unnecessarily. Besides this the lack of perfect agreement between Finn's oaths and the terms he proposed is only an argument *ex silentio* which proves nothing in itself. Nothing forces us to believe that the statement of the terms offered by Finn is exhaustive, while much suggests that it is only a selection. The statement says nothing, *e.g.* about the Danes renouncing their undoubted claim to avenge their lord, yet they must have been expected to bind themselves to forgive and forget the events of the immediate past as a guarantee of future loyalty to Finn[1].

The probability is consequently that Finn ratified the treaty by confirming in his oath what was in the treaty and nothing more, and this probability must be made the basis of further reasoning unless it can be shown to be contradicted by the text or by a reasonable elucidation of the poet's motives as a reporter of the events. If my interpretation of ll. 1096 *b*–97 is correct it certainly confirms this probability; I have therefore still to answer the question raised above about the poet's motives. Why did he consider it insufficient to say merely that both sides ratified the treaty?

The first attempt at an answer might be that there was something unusual in Finn's oath-taking corresponding to the exceptional nature of the circumstances. This might have been so but I do not know sufficiently well what was customary at those times to be able to decide. But, assuming the more difficult case that there was here nothing out of the ordinary, the poet may have had his own reasons for emphasizing Finn's oaths.

In the first place he was obviously concerned with Finn's

[1] That the Danes gave pledges is also the opinion of Lawrence, *Pub. Mod. Lang. Ass. of America*, xxx, No. 2, p. 390.

motives as a negotiator and peace-maker. Now, if I am right in arguing that Finn had the Danes in his power, his offer of terms was a very fair one, guaranteeing as it did the security of his opponents and insisting, not on a complete surrender by them of the stake at issue (whatever it was), but only on a sharing with the Frisians. Supposing that the poet, when he mentioned this offer to treat, had in mind mainly its fairness, it would be natural for him to bring out the points he actually mentions, as proof of this, even if he passed over other contents of the treaty. But Finn's offer, though fair, might be only a ruse to get the Danes out of the hall and into his power. Finn had therefore to be shown not merely as the tactful proposer but as the kingly ratifier of his treaty, frankly pledging his honour in person to Hengest to carry it out[1]. The two moments, then, beginning and end of the negotiations, were equally important to an author to whom Finn was not a mere lay figure, but a human being moving in stirring surroundings with the dramatic gesture that befitted the occasion. Besides, the treaty itself had to be reported, not necessarily in detail but in all its significant points. A little reflection I think is all that is necessary to see that a very effective way to combine this necessity with the former one of showing Finn both as opener and closer of the negotiations was to divide the report of the contents between the beginning and the end of the negotiations: to tell us what in those contents had most significance, at the precise moment when that significance could be best appreciated. What best displays Finn's fairness comes therefore at the beginning; what best shows his royal determination to abide by his proposals comes at the end.

> 1098   þæt he þa wea-lafe   weotena dome
>   arum heolde,

On the basis of the foregoing considerations I hold that the mention of the *wea-laf* here proves that it was referred to

---

[1] A comparison with the tale of Theuderic and Munderic above will illustrate this point. The latter is slain before he comes into the king's presence.

in the treaty offered by Finn; thus we have confirmation of my interpretation of *healfre* in l. 1087. It is requisite, however, to show that there is harmony in the phrasing of the two passages thus connected.

There is the apparent discrepancy here that Finn swears to hold the *wea-laf* honourably, whereas according to the treaty he was only to dispose of one half of it. Obviously his oath implies that the whole *wea-laf* is to pass into his keeping. The explanation lies in the limitation *weotena dome*. Finn is indeed to hold the *wea-laf*, but not *selfes dome*[1], *i.e.* he is not to have full control of it, but must conform to the decisions of a council watching over the use he makes of his power.

The position evidently is that Hengest's holding of the *wea-laf* is transferred to Finn, but the latter does not therewith obtain full power of control and disposal. This the treaty assigns as to one half to Finn, as to the other to Hengest, and the balance between the two is to be kept by the *weotan*, whose office doubtless will be to watch that Finn does not exceed his powers. By swearing to hold honourably, subject to the decision of the *weotan*, Finn confirms the limitation placed by the treaty provisions on his *geweald*.

Undoubtedly everything that had been in the keeping of Hengest *must* pass into the hands of Finn, since the latter becomes the *beag-gyfa* of the Danes. This is the reason why the poet in stating the terms offered to the Danes need say nothing about the "holding" of the *wea-laf*, since it is implicit in the tenour of the treaty that it must change hands, but only mentions (ll. 1087–88) the most important particular, the equal share of both parties in its control, which of course is conceded by the original holders through their acceptance of the proffered terms. The most important gains that could pass into Finn's "holding" in pursuance of the treaty would be vassals and treasure. To either of these the phrase *arum healdan* would apply. Consequently we have still no positive indication of what the *wea-laf* denotes. But it is time to enquire whether we have such of a negative nature.

[1] Cp. ll. 895–6.

The *wea-laf* is directly mentioned twice, here and in l. 1084, and, as we have seen, indirectly once, in l. 1087.

On the first occasion[1] we narrowed down the possibilities of *wea-laf* having a personal reference to one, namely, the possibility that it could denote "survivors on the Danish side." The present mention of the *wea-laf*, in the oath, could be harmonized with this meaning, but it also has a direct reference, as I have shown, to l. 1087. The question therefore is, whether the postulated meaning can be read into l. 1087. Assuming it to be so we should obviously have to understand that Finn, in offering terms to the Danes, declared his readiness to be content with the *geweald* over one half of their number, *i.e.* a divided control over their services, when they became his retainers.

If we ask ourselves, however, whether it is likely that Finn would take his late opponents as a body into his vassalage with the distinct understanding that they were to be as well treated as his own retainers, while at the same time he conceded that he was not to have full control of their movements, the answer must be in the negative. Finn was, as ll. 1099 *b*–1106 show, quite conscious of the dangers that attended the addition to his establishment. He knew also that the Danes would only consent to the proposed arrangement because they were forced by circumstances to do so, *i.e.* because he had them in the long run fully in his power. That in such circumstances he would sacrifice any of the control, which was the only effective guarantee of his own safety in face of men who had a dead chief to avenge, is very improbable. We must, therefore, I believe, rule out the last possibility of *wea-laf* having a personal reference. It can only in the context denote a thing, and what sort of thing I shall try later to establish.

From this it follows that the curious agreement noted on p. 47, namely, between the hypothesis of the *wea-laf* being Danish survivors and the subsequent situation in which Hengest is separated from his followers, is mere coincidence.

[1] See p. 46 f.

This coincidence came about quite naturally, as we shall later see[1].

1099 *b*   þæt ðær ænig mon
      wordum ne worcum   wære ne bræce,
      ne þurh inwit-searo   æfre gemænden,
      ðeah hie hira beag-gyfan   banan folgedon
      ðeoden-lease,   þa him swa geþearfod wæs;

It has been suggested that *þæt* in 1099 *b* can mean "on condition that."[2] If, however, the oath-taking, as we have decided, is not part of the negotiations about the treaty, but of the ceremony which brings the treaty into force, it is most unlikely that Finn would venture to make his performance dependent on further conditions. What would be the use of an oath that *he* would observe one clause of the treaty on condition that no one broke the peace? It is plain here that he undertakes to prevent or to punish such breaches, as would operate against some clause being carried out.

The plural verb in l. 1101 compared with the singular in the preceding line suggests that the *ne* clause is disjunctive; he swore that neither should any man break the peace there (*i.e.* on the side of the one party), nor should they (of the other party) maliciously do so-and-so. This is possible since Finn is to be lord of both parties. It is, however, likewise possible that the subject of the two verbs is the same and the change in number simply a consequence of the fact that logically "no man" is the same as "no men," whence either the poet or the scribe may have forgotten in the second of the clauses that the grammatical subject was in the singular[3]. There is, however, a circumstance which speaks so strongly against the probability of the first of these two alternatives being true, that I think we may reject it. It is this, that Finn only undertakes to impose the penalty of death on a breach of the peace by the Frisians. It is difficult to suppose that Finn would swear to prevent a breach of peace by two con-

---

[1] Below, p. 86 f.   [2] See Chambers' note to l. 1101.
[3] Or the case may be the same as already noted, cp. above, p. 49, my remark on change of number.

tracting parties and not make the penalty the same for both; or, if he intended it to be the same for both, would not say[1], "if then any one of either party call to mind the past" rather than "if any one of the Frisians." Consequently ll. 1099–1101 do not contain two disjunctive clauses: Finn swears to prevent a breach of the peace by one party, the only one which he in fact represents in the negotiations, viz. the Frisians. He undertakes that there shall be no open breach nor one *þurh inwit-searo*, and what that means is clear from what follows[2]: the Frisians are not to irritate the Danes with taunts. Since Finn is speaking for his own party, *gemænden* cannot mean "bemoan," it must have the sense of "advert to, call to mind, make public mention of." For reasons explained in another place[3] I take *þa him swa geþearfod wæs* to mean "since they were admittedly under compulsion." Finn undertakes that no Frisian shall remind the Danes of the past by mentioning the treaty, by which the latter undertook to renounce revenge for their slaughtered lord (the object of *gemænden* is to be supplied from the preceding line); at the same time he tactfully recognizes that they are acting obviously under stress of necessity and that consequently no one has a right to cast up to them their behaviour.

1104   gyf þonne Frysna hwylc   frecnan spræce
     ðæs morþor-hetes   myndgiend wære,
     þonne hit sweordes ecg   syððan scolde.

Finn swears for himself and for the party he represents that the Danes need fear no reminders of the humiliation imposed on them as the natural consequence of their tragic situation. But an oath sworn by a representative is not always felt as binding by the individuals he represents. If someone swears *for* me it has certainly not the same inhibitive force on my actions as if I swore myself. There is always the danger that some individual Frisian (*Frysna hwylc*) may forget that his personal honour is pledged by the oath his king took for

---

[1] Cp. l. 1104.
[3] Cp. p. 94 *n*.
[2] Cp. remark on ll. 1104–06.

all. Hence the necessity to remind the Frisians that the oath taken by the king is not merely a royal promise but a law for all his followers, which entails the severest penalty if broken. Since this legal force of the king's promise is at the same time a guarantee to the Danes, the penalty naturally appears in the formula of his oath.

The formal difficulties of the above lines fortunately do not affect the sense, which is quite clear. Certain breaches of the peace by the Frisians are subject to the death-penalty, to be exacted by their own ruler. A Frisian who taunts a Dane is outside the law of his own country, and cannot claim the support of his countrymen in such a quarrel. The objection of Trautmann[1] to both the form and sense of *frecnan* is groundless. The weak ending is supported by *gleawan spræce*[2] and the sense of "dangerous speech" is quite clear from what precedes; it includes both overt and covert[3] references to the result of the negotiations. A formalist might object that the penalty is only attached to breaches by word of mouth, and does not cover therefore everything mentioned in the *wordum ne worcum* of l. 1100; but in the circumstances obtaining words are most to be feared, and are practically certain to precede deeds.

As regards l. 1106 my anxiety to save the text[4] leads me to make what will no doubt appear a very daring suggestion, but one which may, for all that, prove to deserve consideration. I propose to regard neither *hit* nor *sweordes ecg* as accusative but to take both as nominative. The ellipsis of the infinitive is so frequent with *sceal* when the verb to be understood is intransitive, that it is worth while trying whether we can make sense of the line, as it stands, from this standpoint. I believe we can, for if we take *sweordes ecg* as a metaphor for violent death, which is not a risky proceeding in itself, we get the meaning: "then it should be death afterwards (sc. for the offender)." In Modern English a statement like "If

---

[1] *Bonner Beiträge*, VII, 19.   [2] *Gen.* 2296; cp. *Sprachsch.* under *reord*.
[3] Cp. *þurh inwit-searo*, l. 1101.
[4] Schücking (*E. St.* XLII, 109) has already offered a not very convincing suggestion in this direction.

you do that, it will be sudden death" would be nothing out of the ordinary in colloquial intercourse, and proves at any rate the *a priori* possibility of such a construction. If, however, the double ellipse (of the infinitive and a dative of the person affected) assumed above, seem a too forcible proceeding, I would suggest the small alteration of *hit* to *him*. In that case *þonne him sweordes ecg syððan scolde* would have a parallel in l. 1783, *unc sceal worn fela maþma gemænra, siþðan morgen bið*. The meaning would be, "then the death-penalty should afterwards be his," or perhaps better, in view of the emphatic position of *syððan*, which plainly suggests a nuance of meaning, "then the consequence to him should be the death-penalty."

> 1107   Að wæs geæfned,   ond icge gold
> ahæfen of horde.

A formal difficulty has been perceived here in the singular *að* compared with *aðum benemde* (l. 1097), quite unnecessarily however. The variation between *að* and *aðas* is no more surprising than that between *word* (singular) and *word* (plural), compare the common *worde* or *wordum cweðan*. Compare also *Orosius* (Sweet), 162, 10, *þa oðsworan hie þæm ærendracan mid þæm bismerlicestan aðe þæt hie...þeh þe þa aðas wæren near mane þonne soðe.*

The raising of the gold from the treasure can hardly be a mere ornamental detail; of such the concise style of this précis hardly permits. Like every other circumstance mentioned it must have a significant place in the chain of events. But what is that place? Is the production of the gold consequent on the completion of the ceremony of oath-taking? Or is it part of the preparations for the cremation of Hnæf?

Hord and *rice* are associated together (l. 3004, cp. l. 912, *hord ond hleo-burh, hæleþa rice, eðel Scyldinga*); the treasure goes with and is a symbol of sovereignty. There can be no doubt that *this* treasure belonged to a sovereign personage, either Finn or Hnæf, but to which of the two? We can reply that if the raising of gold from the treasure was to give effect to the treaty, it might *a priori* have belonged either to Finn or Hnæf, but if it was part of the preparation for Hnæf's cremation it could only have belonged to Hnæf. Can we assign it to Hnæf on the last of these grounds? In other words, is it probable that gold from Hnæf's treasure was laid on his pyre? The treasure of a king was held for others, not as purely personal property; this comes out in the high appreciation of kingly generosity. Along with his sovereignty it passed on to his heirs (cp. ll. 910–913). It cannot, therefore, have been usual to sacrifice regal treasure at the funeral pyre of a king. The suggested burning of the dragon's treasure after Beowulf's death was plainly altogether exceptional and contrasts strongly with the hero's dying thanks to God that he had won such riches for his people (ll. 2794–98). It was obviously a measure which could only be carried out by the people acting as a whole, and furthermore, as the speech of the messenger (ll. 2900 ff.) shows, was a counsel of despair. Consequently it would be the duty of the small band which had accompanied Hnæf to Finn's court to preserve his treasure intact so far as lay in their power. If it did not lie in their power, that would be because the treasure had passed into Finn's hands, and this could only have been a consequence of the treaty. Furthermore it is noticeable that in the enumeration of the costly articles visible on the pyre only armour is mentioned (gilded helm and bloody corslet). Doubtless the terror of the scene rather than its magnificence is in the poet's mind, and he might have felt that the treasure gold once mentioned needed no further emphasis. But if Hnæf's retainers, the *ðeoden-lease*, now the humiliated followers of their chieftain's slayer, still possessed the power and the will to sacrifice even a part of his treasure on the pyre, that circumstance would psychologically be so important as to call for more than a vague passing reference, especially when we consider that the pyre scene is treated by the poet with "elegiac expansion."[1] Furthermore, ll. 1107–08 *a* are the transition from the negotiations to the funeral ceremonies.

---

[1] Cp. above, p. 17.

They may contain the last act of the former and the first step in the latter. The *ond* may denote the association in the poet's mind of the last of one series of events with the first of the next following. Then the words would have the force, "they ratified the treaty and had leisure to think of preparations for the funeral." But can *að wæs geæfned* here have the sense of "they ratified the treaty (or, completed its ratification)"? Gering translates "Der Schwur ward geleistet." But should it not rather be "Der Schwur war geleistet"? Is that not clear when we take together *Fin...aðum benemde* with the obvious transition to something else: *að wæs geæfned, i.e.* the oath-taking was over and done with? The episode of the negotiations is past: the poet introduces a new scene and sums up significant traits in the situation; narrative gives way to description. The oaths had been sworn, gold had been raised from the hoard, Hnæf's corpse had been prepared for the funeral rites, the mourning survivors were collected round the pyre, with its grisly reminders of slaughter. Then Hildeburh emerges once more to view and the narrative begins afresh. If we now return to the syntactical form of the text, there can be little doubt that the *ond* of l. 1107 denotes a closer association in the poet's mind of the raising of the gold with the oath-taking than with the getting ready of Hnæf's corpse for the last rites. Oath-taking and gold-raising are plainly in his thought co-ordinate parts of a whole distinct from the funeral preparations; they are the two completed acts in the ratification of the treaty. Taken together they denote that the treaty had been finally ratified, and the way cleared for the common celebration of the funeral ceremonies for the fallen on both sides, to which the poet now addresses himself.

If now the gold-raising must be regarded as an act in the ratification of the treaty, in other words a payment made by one side to the other, it becomes considerably easier to decide whether Frisian or Danish treasure is meant, since there can be little hesitation as to which side is indicated as payer by the situation. Although Finn offered to be a generous lord to the Danes, that undertaking referred not to the conclusion of peace, but to future "ring-spending" in hall, and to occasions when his own vassals were to profit as well as the Danes. On the other hand Hengest, who was to become a vassal of Finn's, would be obliged by Teutonic custom to place his possessions at his new lord's disposal, and since his entrance into Finn's service was not voluntary, the paying over of any treasure he held would also be forced, *i.e.* provided for in the terms of the treaty. That being so, we can understand why the poet passes over Hengest's share in the oath-taking; the most significant act he had to perform in ratifying the treaty was to pay up.

The attentive reader will probably have noticed that the argument about the hoard is convergent with that I have pursued about the *wea-laf*. Regarding the latter, I have sought to establish against common opinion that it is a thing, without as yet deciding what thing. It is apparent, however, that the word in its literal meaning ("leavings of disaster") might easily refer to a treasure which played a rôle in tragic vicissitudes such as are obviously present in the Finn Saga, and it is noticeable that the indications we have collected concerning it harmonize with those just gained about the hoard. As regards the *wea-laf* we have learned the following:

(1) It was held by Hengest at the moment when hostilities were broken off.

(2) Finn desired its possession.

(3) In the treaty Finn proposed a clause by which, (*a*) the half-control of it was to be abandoned to him, (*b*) he was in return to put Frisians and Danes on an equal footing as regards claims on his generosity.

(4) Finn swore in ratification of the treaty to hold it in accordance with the decisions of a council.

We therefore now know, on the one hand, that by treaty something of great price was to pass from Hengest's keeping into Finn's; on the other hand, that the treaty was ratified by a payment made from Danish treasure, presumably by the leader of the Danes, *i.e.* Hengest. Given these premisses the inference that the *wea-laf* is the hoard is unavoidable.

It should also be noticed that Finn's readiness to give the Danes equal claims on his generosity with the Frisians in return for something conceded by the Danes, in itself makes strong presumption that this something is treasure. Finn could hardly expect his own vassals to share equally with their late opponents unless his resources were being increased by a contribution from the latter.

Hengest as the king's thane (l. 1085) can hardly have been the original owner of the treasure. That must have belonged to the king, but when Hnæf fell fighting his treasure would, of course, pass to the keeping of the person who succeeded him as leader of the Danes. That Hnæf should have taken his hoard abroad with him may seem strange to modern eyes, but was a natural proceeding in the days when a man's treasure was as inseparable from his person as his weapons.

Of all the attempts to solve the riddle presented by the mysterious *icge* of l. 1107 the only one which seems to me to be at all promising is that which connects it with the *incge* of l. 2577, and refers both, following Thorpe, to a proper name. In view of the fact that objects of value are so frequently denoted in *Beowulf* as inherited from predecessors, this proceeding has a fair *a priori* likelihood. As the starting-point I would suggest a genitive plural *Inga*. If it is true that the old name for a division of the Germanic tribes, **Ingwai-waniz*, permits us to infer a shorter form, viz. **Ingwōz*[1], there is a fair presumption that this might have survived into Old English either as an alternative form to *Ingwine* or independently. *Inga gold = Ingwina gold, i.e.* "gold of the Danes," would suit well enough in l. 1107, but in this case it looks suspicious that both here and in l. 2577 the ending should appear as *-e*. It seems unlikely that on two occasions a scribe would fail to recognize a genitive plural even if he did not understand the word. On the other hand if it had once been usual to designate valuables as derived from a race of legendary half-forgotten forefathers called the *Ingas*, the genitive plural might have survived simply as an indeclinable adjective used

[1] Cp. Helm, *Altgermanische Religionsgeschichte*, I, 333.

to denote that things were of great dignity or very valuable (cp. the analogous development in the case of Old High Germ. *frôno*), even after the *Ingas* themselves had been forgotten[1]. In this case the ending might by analogy be transformed to equate with normal stem-forms, so that *inga gold, laf* would become *inge gold, laf.*

It is however perhaps not necessary to operate with an old genitive in order to arrive at the stem-form *inge-.* According to Bremer[2] the stem **Ingwia-* (cp. Inguiomerus) is certain. In that case the equation, *incge-laf* : *eormen-laf* :: *Inguaeones* : *Herminones*, becomes suggestive. Remains the difficulty of deciding on a meaning for *Ingwia-/inge.* The problem of its precise meaning, so far as I see practically insoluble, is however not of great importance. It is certain, whatever it meant, that it would belong to a class of words expressing excellence or value. Of course all this is extremely hypothetical. But a hypothesis which enables us to preserve one historically attested form (the *incge* in *incge lafe*) instead of replacing it by uncertain conjecture, and at the same time enables us to emend the altogether doubtful *icge* with the minimum of change in the passage where it occurs, is worth having.

1113 b   sume on wæle crungon.

Klaeber's important discovery that *sume* is litotes, throws a flood of light. Since *lyt* is the common form of understatement for "none," it is clear that *sum* as understatement must denote "all," if we accept the equation:—none: few=all: some (cp. "few or none," "some or all"). It is therefore said of the dead who were visible on the pyre that all had perished in the fight. The pyre was intended for those who fell fighting.

---

[1] We might even do without these highly hypothetical Ingas in view of Old Norse *ingi*, "princeps," which would bring the postulated gen. plur. still nearer in meaning to *frôno*. Cp. Loewenthal, *PBB.* XLVII, 272.

[2] *Ethnographie der germanischen Stämme*, § 81, note 1 = *Pauls Grundriss*, (2nd ed.), III, 813.

1114   Het ða Hildeburh   æt Hnæfes ade
       hire selfre sunu   sweoloðe befæstan,
       ban-fatu bærnan   ond on bæl don;

At first sight *sunu* contradicts the *bearnum* of l. 1074, which as I pointed out is probably a real plural. It should be noted, however, that both forms might possibly be correct, since Finn might well be wedded to Hildeburh *en secondes noces* and his family consist of one son by Hildeburh and one or more by his first wife. Then the *bearn* of l. 1074 might include Hildeburh's own son and her stepsons: *selfre*, which rhymes, may quite possibly have the emphasis which would imply a distinction of this sort. Inconclusive is also Cosijn's argument that *ban-fatu* proves *sunu* to be (an Anglian) plural. Reversing the illogical order of the verbs in l. 1116 we can translate "Taking her stand at Hnæf's pyre Hildeburh gave the order to commit her own son to the flames, to put the bodies in the blaze (or, to set the bodies ablaze?) and burn them." That is to say, the poet may well have conceived the scene so, that Hildeburh, having ordered her son to be laid on the pyre, likewise gave the signal to kindle the fire which was to consume all[1]. The fact that an order from Hildeburh is required before her son's body is laid on the pyre suggests strongly that there is something unusual or unexpected here. Two hypotheses might account for this. One is, that Hildeburh's son did not fall in the fight, that he was too young to be a warrior and came by his death in some other way than the honourable one of falling in battle. In that case he would, of course, not belong to the company for whom the pyre was intended, and only the mother's passionate love would claim for his corpse the honours extended to his seniors. The other hypothesis is, that there were two pyres, one for the Frisians and one for the Danes, and that the poet's sympathies led him only to mention the latter one. In this case Hildeburh would give expression to her natural clan feeling in ordering

---

[1] Of course there may be a possibility that *ban-fatu* is a collective plural meaning "limbs." This would simplify the matter, but it is better to face the more difficult problem.

her son to be laid on his uncle's pyre, rather than on that one which was destined for the Frisian princes and vassals.

On the whole, the first hypothesis is more probable, since it would be natural that in the common celebration of the funeral rites one pyre should be erected for all as symbol of the reunion of the two parties concerned. It would likewise be natural to call this "Hnæf's pyre," as he was the person of supreme rank among the fallen. If this reckoning is right we may here have a hint of the following order of events: firstly, the death of Hildeburh's little son; then, an outburst of strife between the Frisians and the Danes, in which further sons of Finn are slain as well as his vassals and, on the other side, Hnæf (and his brothers?). Cp. my reconstruction of the Saga (p. 122 f. below).

> 1117   earme on eaxle   ides gnornode,
>   geomrode giddum.   Guð-rinc astah.

These lines are sufficiently difficult to excuse attempts at emendation and Holthausen's ingenious *eame* for *earme* has enjoyed a certain popularity. Still, recent editors seem to be unanimous in leaving the text as it stands, even Chambers who regards Holthausen's suggestion as "very probable." This shows in my opinion a healthy instinct, and I content myself with trying to explain the manuscript reading.

It is characteristic of the poet's style that he often introduces a descriptive or explanatory remark at a point where to us it seems to come too late, *i.e. after* something which it ought to have *preceded*. This gives such remarks a parenthetic effect and they are often enclosed by editors in brackets. The phenomenon is especially noticeable after a "kwath," cp. characteristic examples at the following places, ll. 2632, 2725, 405. It would appear that when the poet pictured to himself one of his persons as speaking, he had a tendency, as it were, to take a retrospective or diagnostic view of this personage, and to interpolate between the announcement of his beginning to speak and the report of what he said, the result of such retrospect or diagnosis. Now of course the present instance is not on all fours with the illustrations I have quoted. But the poet does think of Hildeburh as saying something though he does not put a speech in her mouth, and if he had the tendency just noted in one class of instances, it might assert itself occasionally in another class not very different. That would likely be so if his progress were a little more hurried than usual, and we have already seen that in the Episode there is a change in his manner in this direction. I suggest, therefore, that ll. 1116–17 *a* are parenthetic in the above sense, and really are intended to show concretely in what state of mind Hildeburh was at the moment of giving the order— she *had* till then been lying on her dead son's shoulder mourning and pouring forth her plaints. If this be so, we can take the ascension of the warrior as following directly on the command, and in that case it is likely the action of the person who obeys the command and ascends the pile to lay the additional body on it—the last, evidently unrehearsed, incident in the preparations, and immediately followed by the conflagration.

One advantage of the hypothesis just advanced is that it enables us to take *Guð-rinc astah* in its literal sense. Otherwise, so long as we do not wish to assume the responsibility of an emendation, we are forced to understand these words in a figurative sense referring to a corpse that was laid on the pyre. If we do this we are landed in two serious difficulties.

Firstly, although the Old Norse parallel discovered by Bugge (*áðr á bál stigi = áðr hann væri á bál borinn*) proves that a phrase like "to ascend the pyre" could be used as a figure for "to be laid on the pyre," it seems unlikely that in this figurative use the phrase would be reduced to "to ascend" (leaving the necessary enlargement to be inferred). Boer's objection[1], "dass bei dieser interpretation *on bæl* unentbehrlich wäre," is perhaps exaggerated, but it does seem to be the case that figurative phrases are not often reduced in this way unless when they are in very frequent use. Now in the absence of parallels we cannot know that this particular idiom

---

[1] *Zs. für deutsches Altertum*, XLVII, 135.

was a common one in Anglo-Saxon. Secondly, to speak at one and the same time of a corpse both in a literal way and in a figurative way that logically contradicts the first, is an inconcinnity which one is loth to ascribe to an author unless there is no other alternative. However we translate, it is here a question of a corpse, which is clearly indicated as such, and to say that this "ascended" is logically to attribute to it a power of movement which it could not possess. No doubt such mingling of contradictory standpoints is *possible* under almost any circumstances, but when we are dealing with the description of a concrete situation it only becomes *probable* on the assumption that the author had not clearly visualized the scene, or suddenly ceased to do so. If the poet actually pictured to himself Hildeburh mourning recumbent on the lifeless body of her son till it was taken from her and laid on the pyre at her own behest, he could hardly say (I opine) that the body "ascended." On the other hand, if he did thus picture the scene in vivid outline, he might for the abstract statement: "The warrior to whom she addressed herself obeyed her command," substitute the concrete trait: "The warrior ascended," which challenges the imagination by its laconic nature, and forces the hearer to *see*, if he will understand.

1121 *b*   ðonne blod ætspranc
      laÞ-bite lices.

If *laÞ-bite* really means "wound" it would probably be better to take it, as Schücking proposed[1], as variant of *ben-geato* in l. 1121 *a*. A good deal turns however on whether we have to take *bite* as denoting the action of biting or its result. In the two instances in which the simplex occurs in *Beowulf* the word means "biting." As *laÞ* seems generally to denote something which is actively inimical or injurious, the probability is perhaps that *laÞ-bite* means "hostile biting." We might then perhaps regard its form as being a comitative dative, of the sort that I assumed above, p. 19. Colloquially

---

[1] *E. St.* XLII, 110.

we often denote a causally related idea in Modern English as *comitative*, by means of *with*, *e.g.* we can say, "The wall has crumbled with the weather." Perhaps the literal meaning here is "then the blood sprang forth with the biting of the body (by the flames)"—understanding *lices* of course as objective genitive. If we follow Schücking, *ðonne* must be taken as conjunction, which seems to me here stylistically unpleasing—an unbroken series of sharp asyndetic statements has a better descriptive effect. The spouting of the blood should hardly be reduced to a mere accompanying circumstance.

> 1125   Gewiton him ða wigend   wica neosian
>   freondum befeallen,   Frysland geseon,
>   hamas ond hea-burh.

The literal meaning of these lines is clear enough, apart from the fact that there is some confusion about *hea-burh*. This is translated by some as "chief city, capital." What evidence is there, however, that *burg* is ever used in the meaning of "town" or "city" by the poet of *Beowulf*?

The original meaning of *burg* is of course "fortified place, stronghold."[1] In process of time this developed in England into the meaning "town or city," but this can hardly have taken place before the Anglo-Saxons became themselves town-dwellers. Till that took place they might indeed apply the word *burg* to a Roman city, but this would not be because it meant "city" to them, but because such a city was a stronghold. Even allowing however that the Anglo-Saxons had already made the transition to town life when the *Beowulf* was composed, how much reason is there to suppose that the poet pictured to himself the continental Teutons of an earlier day as living in towns? It is clear that tradition had preserved a vivid picture of former conditions, so vivid indeed that it must in the main have been faithful to fact. Is it likely then that the Frisians appeared to our poet as town-dwellers, the Friesland of Finn's day as a country dotted over with towns, of which one was the capital of the kingdom?

[1] Cp. Schuchardt on *burg* in Hoops' *Reallexikon*.

There is of course no compulsion at all to take *hea(h)* in composition with *burg* as meaning " chief." The "lofty" *burg* may well have been the chieftain's *heall* (a stronghold within the stronghold) which reared itself high above the humbler dwelling-places that gathered around it in the enclosed space of the fortifications[1]. The *hamas ond hea-burh* together would then make up the *burg* as a whole, and it is hence not surprising that the whole collection is often denoted by *burg* in the plural.

Though however the literal sense of the passage is clear enough, as also its function in the economy of the narrative (it introduces the situation of affairs which is a result of the conclusion of the treaty), when we try to form a clear and definite picture of the movements of the warriors to whom it refers certain difficulties arise. In the first place we have the question about the starting-point of those movements. The going of the warriors "to see Friesland" certainly suggests to a modern reader that the meeting-place of l. 1082 was not in Friesland, that the stronghold of Finn where the fighting and subsequent negotiations took place lay outside the Frisian kingdom. This was Bugge's view and it has been strongly upheld recently by Chambers[2] against Klaeber.

It would certainly be rather surprising if we were forced to believe that Finn's residence, *þær he ær mæste heold worolde wynne*, lay outside his own country, for this would imply that the king of Friesland was a regular absentee from his own dominions. He might, indeed, after conquering the country of another clan have taken up his residence among them, but to assume this on the sole evidence of one phrase alone is going too far unless it be proved that the phrase could only convey what it seems to a modern reader to imply. The phrase may have implied something different, and that it actually did so Klaeber tried to establish by a parallel from *The Battle of Brunanburh*, l. 53, *Gewitan him þa Norðmenn... Dyflen secean, and eft Iraland*. According to Klaeber if we infer from *Beowulf*, l. 1126, that Finn's burg lay outside

[1] Cp. the description of Heorot, ll. 81 *b*–82 *a*.
[2] *Introduction to Beowulf*, p. 258, n. 4.

Friesland then we must infer from the passage just quoted that Dublin was not in Ireland. The reason he says so is evidently that he takes the passage to mean "The Northmen went to Dublin and then on to Ireland," for, accepting this to be the meaning, it results that the Anglo-Saxon speaker could talk of "going to seek Ireland from Dublin," *i.e.* could conceive Dublin as a starting-point for visiting Ireland, and consequently Finn's burg as a starting-point for seeing Friesland even if it were in Friesland. Klaeber's inference is certainly correct, if the above be the only possible meaning of the Brunanburh passage. But *eft* is a somewhat ambiguous word: it can mean *iterum*, *denuo* or *retro*, *rursus*. We have a choice between translating: "The Northmen went to Dublin and on to Ireland" or "They went to Dublin, back to Ireland." Chambers evidently understands the latter, for he denies vigorously Klaeber's inference, which certainly does not follow unless we take *eft* here to mean *iterum*. So far as I see it is not to be made out with certainty whether the poet of the *Battle of Brunanburh* regarded the going to Dublin and Ireland as successive items in the journey of the North-men or as two ways of saying the same thing. Klaeber's parallel cannot in my opinion be taken as decisive of the meaning of *Frysland geseon*. On the other hand, its failure to establish what Klaeber wished to prove, by no means disposes of the possibility that *Frysland geseon* did not necessarily imply what modern readers tend to take out of it. From what follows it appears likely that Finn's burg was situated on or in close proximity to the coast. If the poet was thinking of the Danes removing from the king's hall to go further afield, he may have had it in his mind that all was new to them as recent arrivals, and therefore that they actually were seeing Friesland for the first time, although they had landed on its coast some time before. From this it is evident that our view of what this phrase implies depends on the reference we give to *wigend*. Meeting us, as this word does, immediately after the poet's comment on the great losses on both sides (1. 1124), we naturally tend to take it as a collective reference to all the warriors engaged. In this case we understand the poet to tell us that, peace and the common celebration of funeral rites having been concluded, the assembled forces were dismissed to their quarters in Friesland, namely, another burg (or, as some will have it, the capital). But reflection on the implications contained in this is not reassuring as to its correctness. We are prepared, indeed, to learn that the Danes marched off to that *oðer flet* which had been assigned them by treaty, but this manoeuvre we do not expect to find mixed up with the movements of the Frisian troops, who, if they left Finn's burg at all, would presumably on the return of peace be dismissed each man to his own home. It is certainly unexpected if we are here only to be told that there was a general break-up, and nothing more, thus leaving us to imply that the occupation of the *oðer flet* was a necessary incident of the resultant movements, which did not require special mention. It is, however, difficult to believe that when the poet tells us "The warriors went to their quarters," he indicated thus summarily both that the Frisians went to their home quarters in time of peace and that the Danes went to the new quarters assigned to them by treaty in a foreign land. Nor is it likely that the necessity for compression under which as a précis-writer he was labouring, would lead him to deal with the situation in this fashion. We might expect this, indeed, to lead him to drop every detail which could be left out. But when as here he had the choice between making a confused general statement which applied to two parties in a different sense, and making one which said succinctly what one party actually did, there can be only slight doubt about the result. For he obviously has a choice here. If he tell us that the Danes actually did what they were to be allowed to do, he has said pregnantly all that is necessary to introduce the situation wrought by the treaty. He does not need to mention the Frisian troops. They are in their own country and we naturally assume that on the return of peace they betake themselves to peaceful occupations. If we see the Danes actually settled in the *oðer flet*, we have all the imagination requires, in order to construct the background for what follows.

Looking once more at our passage in the light of these considerations, it strikes one that, as a *whole*, it is much less general than its opening statement. There is a successive narrowing of the predicate. The warriors went to their quarters, namely, (1) in Friesland (not also in the Half-Danes' country, as Binz pointed out[1]), (2) at the *hea-burh*. The whole statement is therefore, "the warriors went to the *hea-burh*." Now by the treaty, the Danes were not to go home but to take up their quarters in a castle containing a *healle ond heah-setl*, *i.e.* in a (Frisian) *hea-burh*, and they were to occupy this by themselves. The Danes and Frisians cannot therefore have gone to the same *hea-burh*, and if only one party is referred to, it is obviously not the Frisians.

It seems possible also that there is a limitation of the subject expressed. *Freondum befeallen* certainly describes a high degree of destitution which would hardly apply to the Frisians as long as their *hleo* Finn is alive.

Having got thus far in our reasoning, it becomes a matter of indifference whether Finn's burg is inside Friesland or not. The points of importance are that (1) the Danes evacuate the hall they had defended; (2) they do not go to their ships[2] but are sent into Friesland, which allows us to presume that their new quarters have an inland position at some distance from the sea, as might be expected since Finn would hardly wish to make it easy for them to escape; (3) Finn's burg is not vacated by him, but by implication continues to be his residence after he has reoccupied his hall[3].

> 1127 *b*   Hengest ða gyt
>   wæl-fagne winter   wunode mid Finnel
>   unhlitme;

Here the textual problem must first be dealt with. The word *unhlitme* does not fill a half-line, hence a word is missing. This

---

[1] *Zs. f. d. Ph.* XXXVII, 532.   [2] Cp. l. 1130.

[3] This last point is confirmed by l. 1147, for *his selfes ham* must be the place *þær he ær mæste heold worolde wynne*.

proves that the inorganic *l* of *Finnel* is probably due to two successive words coalescing, a species of mistake which is not likely to be made with the eye. It is therefore probable that the scribe read the whole sentence, or the last clause of it. and proceeded to write it down from memory, guiding himself as he did so by the sound of the syllables, rather than by visualizing the written forms. Now in the spoken form of a sentence two words could easily coalesce if the first ended and the second began with a vowel. Hence the probability that the missing word began with a vowel, which is borne out by the vowel alliteration of l. 1129. Again, since the form *unhlitme* is proved by the alliteration to have the accentuation $\acute{\times} \grave{\times} \times$ (as a compound of *un-* it could only be that or $\times \acute{\times} \times$) the missing word was either a monosyllable beginning with a vowel and ending in *l* or *l* + consonant, or a dissyllable of which the first syllable consisted of a vowel followed by *l*. This reminds us at once of the not far distant half-line *elne unflitme* which the scribe would probably read as *eln' unflitme* and which has also a suitable metrical structure. This *elne* would obviously supply all the above-mentioned conditions, which few other words would do, and gives us accordingly the text *mid Finne elne unhlitme* read by the scribe as *mid Finn' eln' unhlitme*. There still remains the difficulty of explaining the loss of *n* after *l*, which may, however, be attempted as follows. A scribe trained to separate the words as he wrote might indeed depend either regularly or occasionally on his consciousness of the sound of the spoken syllables as an aid to memory and a substitute for too frequent reference to the manuscript in front of him, but he would at the same time try to break up the spoken syllables in writing, wherever necessary to denote the beginning of a word. That is to say he would not group the written signs always in exact concurrence with the spoken syllables. There would, however, obviously be the danger that he might forget to break a syllable where necessary, and this apparently was the case when our scribe wrote *Finnel*. Having done this he would have still on our hypothesis to write down what he spoke as *nun-*

hlitme. Here, however, his orthographical consciousness might awake in time to remind him that *unhlitme* was one word and that in its written form it could not possibly have an *n* prefixed to it. Strictly speaking, he ought of course to have tacked this *n* on to what he had already written, but this apparently he forgot to do with the result that the *n* disappeared altogether.

That this sort of mistake is not very common in decent MSS. is a result of the fact that a practised copyist will not generally rely on the spoken form of words as an aid to his memory for transcription, but rather on his perception of the sense. It is only when his attention is diverted for any reason from the sense that a mistake of this sort is likely to occur. It is probable, therefore, that there was something here which puzzled the *Beowulf* scribe, namely the circumstance that the phrase *elne unhlitme* was foreign to him, and he did not understand it. If that be true, it is likely that he was equally puzzled by *elne unflitme*, since the difficulty of explaining either of these is about equally great to us, and this suggests that the MS. he copied had the same phrase in both places, and that the scribe may have gone wrong twice though in two different ways. If, therefore, we can find an acceptable explanation of either *unhlitme* or *unflitme* which would suit the sense both here and in l. 1097 we should have not inconsiderable justification for emending one of the two accordingly, always assuming, of course, that we can only explain one of them. The analysis of *unhlitme* gives us a stem *hlitm* which can be identified tentatively with the once attested *hlytm*. This, in its turn, in the one place where it occurs[1] can be explained as a derivative from the root of *hleotan*. Since, however, the prefix *un* usually is compounded with noun-stems of abstract meaning, it will be necessary, in order to connect *unhlitme* with *hlytm*, to give to the latter an abstract, instead of the concrete, meaning usually assigned to it (viz. "lot"). There is, however, no particular difficulty about this, since the *m*-suffixes appear in both concrete and abstract

---

[1] *Beowulf,* l. 3126.

nouns[1]. I take *hlytm*, therefore, to mean not "lot" but rather "drawing of lots." The *on hlytme* of l. 3126 will then mean literally "at lot-drawing," *i.e.* "subject to the decision of chance," much the same idea as we express by "on the lap of the gods"; in other words, *on hlytme* conveys that something is not decided, or is yet to be decided. The poet probably says here, "It was not undecided (*i.e.* it was already decided), who should spoil the hoard," and I see in this an allusion to the fact that the Geats owed their opportunity not to their own bravery but to their dead lord.

Turning now to *unhlitme* and taking its form to be that of a dative with the common adverbial function of this case, this would give the meaning "not by drawing lots, *i.e.* not by, or as a consequence of leaving matters to chance"; the word could therefore express that a thing was done in accordance with a previous decision, whether as a result of agreement or other causes would depend on circumstances.

In pursuance of this line of reasoning, I propose that we should see in *elne unhlitme* an asyndetic combination of adverbs[2] meaning "zealously and in accordance with agreement," or "zealously, as had already been arranged."

It now appears that we have the possibility of saving *unflitme* as well as *unhlitme*. After all, an *m*-derivative from the root of *flitan* is just as possible as one from that of *hleotan*[3]: *unflitme* might well mean "without disputation or discussion, *i.e.* without further ado." In this case the two words, so like each other and so different, would really have practically the same meaning, for what is done between two parties without fuss or further ado is generally that which has already been agreed. Both *unhlitme* and *unflitme* may well be remnants of old legal phraseology, expressing readiness to carry out contracts. That such phraseology would naturally occur to the

---

[1] Cp. Kluge, *Stammbildungslehre*, §§ 88, 152–4, and von Bahder, *Verbalabstracta*, p. 129 f.

[2] Such combinations of minor members of a sentence are of course not unusual in Old English. Cp. l. 2573, *þy fyrste forman dogore*; l. 740, *hraðe forman siðe*.

[3] V. Bahder, *loc. cit.* p. 135.

poet when relating what befell at and after the making of peace between the Frisians and the Danes hardly needs to be remarked. Furthermore, the meaning which is common to both is equally suitable in either case where they occur. And after all, that two words should have the same meaning and also agree in their suffix and prefix and in having roots which ended in *t* is not so very surprising, while the explanation given above of the mistake made in l. 1129 makes it rather more probable that a fairly reliable scribe, with a clearly written MS. in front of him, would only be led into error once in such a way, than that he should err twice.

Further formal difficulties scarcely arise in connection with this passage. The winter which Hengest spends with Finn is personified and therefore called *wæl-fag*, which must denote almost the same idea as *morþre gemearcod* in l. 1264; it was a gloomy winter, darkened by the shadow of the catastrophe which had preceded it.

Having disposed of the textual difficulty raised by the MS. reading, we turn now to the meaning of the whole. There can be no doubt of the adversative effect of the statement made here in its relation to the preceding sentence. *Gyt* expresses the continuity of an action or state as unbroken, either in agreement or in contrast with something else expressed or implied. Since the going of the *wigend* in the preceding sentence means a break in continuity, Hengest's staying is here contrasted with it as a continuation in his former position. *They* leave the place where they have hitherto been, Hengest stays behind. *He* remains at Finn's burg while the others go off to the *hea-burh*. As he stays *mid Finne* it is plain that, as we assumed above, Finn does not vacate his castle. Naturally, since the offer of the *oðer flet* was an obvious reflection of his desire to resume uninterrupted sway in his own house.

Since we decided above that the *wigend* were the Danes, we now have the result that Hengest and his men are separated, furthermore this takes place *elne unhlitme*, by agreement. As Hengest would naturally prefer to accompany his own people, this agreement must have come about as a part of Finn's policy during the treaty-making. It will be necessary to devote some attention to it in this light.

It has already been noted that Finn's taking the Danes into his service was attended by risks which he could not ignore and must provide for. It would, therefore, naturally be his policy in carrying out the terms of the treaty to shape their application so as to minimize these risks. Thus, the granting of the occupation of another *flet* to the Danes could be used by assigning them an inland situation where they would be cut off from their natural avenue of escape, the sea; and at the same time could be isolated from continuous intercourse with his own men, by which means the possibility of that friction, which he had sworn to prevent, would be lessened. But it would also be advisable for him to divide the Danes, if possible, from the very enterprising leader who was responsible for the vigorous defence of the hall. If Finn could keep Hengest as a hostage in his immediate neighbourhood under his own personal observation, he would doubtless feel that the Danes in their *hea-burh* were well under control. An excuse to do this would be offered by the treaty clauses which dealt with the *wea-laf*, the treasure. The possession of this passed into Finn's hands when he became lord of the Danes, but, as we have seen, there were stringent conditions governing his disposal of it, and it was provided that this should be subject to the decisions of the *weotan*. On this body the Danes would naturally require to be represented, and who would be the most natural person to act as their representative, if not Hengest? Certainly the Danes would have to leave someone at Finn's court to act for them in this capacity, and we can be sure that Finn at any rate would see to it that this person was Hengest, even supposing that the mere logic of the situation did not designate the Danes' leader as the only candidate for the office.

1129 *b*   eard gemunde,
þeah þe he meahte   on mere drifan
hringed-stefnan.

The positive form of the *þeah* statement is, in view of the ordinary function of the word in *Beowulf*, surprising.

It is usual, therefore, to emend l. 1131 *a* by introducing a *ne*. This, although it brings the sentence formally into line with the instances in which *þeah* introduces a negative statement—*e.g.* l. 1168 ("They credited him with courage in spite of his not being trustworthy in battle")—is not altogether satisfactory, since inability to put to sea is at first sight hardly a reason for not thinking of home[1].

Furthermore, we have no business to emend until it has been proved that the text is impossible. Since Klaeber has shown[2] that the MS. reading is possible and gives a satisfactory sense, Schücking's rejection of the emendation in the last recension of Heyne's edition (1918) deserves approval. I am, however, not satisfied that it is advisable to take *þeah þe* here as a dependent interrogative. A simpler explanation may, I think, be given as follows: Klaeber refers to a group of instances listed in Miss Burnham's study under the title of "Idiomatic instances of the *þeah*-clause."[3] I hold that these permit the inference that the conjunction *þeah* (*þe*) could be employed not only to denote that the content of the principal sentence is opposed to that of the dependent sentence but also to denote, less commonly, that the content of the latter is contradicted by the situation or general likelihood, the *þeah* in this case pointing *outside* the whole sentence to something given as fact or probability. Thus *þonne andwyrdan þa yrfenuman swa he sylf sceolde þeah he lif hæfde* (Then the heirs answered as he himself should supposing he were yet alive—contradiction of fact); *Hwilc wundor wæs, þeah se halga wer ealne middaneard ætforan him gesawe* (What wonder was it, though the holy man saw the whole world before him

---

[1] Cp. Schücking, *Satzverknüpfung*, p. 22.
[2] *Anglia*, Beiblatt XXII, 373.
[3] See Josephine M. Burnham, *Yale Studies in English*, No. XXXIX, pp. 33–4.

—contradiction of ordinary probability); *Forðæm ðu ne þearft nauht swiþe wundrian ðeah we spyrien*...(Therefore you need not be much surprised though we ask—namely, in contradiction to your expectation). As a contradiction of probability I also explain the cases where *þeah þe* is used after *nytan, uncuð, e.g. Ic nat þeah ðu wene þæt*...(I don't know that you may not after all think that...); *uncuð þeah þe he slæpe*...(No one knows that he may not after all be asleep). The point about the last two examples is that "may be" is equivalent to "may not be," and that the Modern English idiom demands the negative where Anglo-Saxon had the positive. Colloquially, however, *but* may be used without a following negative in a function similar to this one of *þeah*, *e.g.* "I don't know but you're right" (*i.e.* I don't know that you may not be right in spite of appearances).

I consider, therefore, that the *þeah þe* denotes here in our context that an expectation of Hengest's was improbable in view of the situation in which he found himself at Finn's castle, and translate: "His thoughts were of home, that he might after all be able to steer his ship over the sea." The subordinate clause explains the principal clause. Hengest was too active a character to have merely sentimental thoughts of home. Such thoughts for him were thoughts of escape.

I remark that it does not seem to me to be in the least necessary to put the description of the sea (ll. 1131 *b*–33 *a*) in brackets, as Schücking does. The obviously intentional symbolic meaning of the landscape is too important to allow it to be buried in a parenthesis. I therefore begin a new sentence, as follows:

1131 *b*   Holm storme weol,
  won wið winde; winter yþe beleac
  is-gebinde, oþ ðæt oþer com
  gear in geardas, swa nu gyt doað,
  þa ðe syngales sele bewitiað,
  wuldor-torhtan weder.

The poetical significance of the winter landscape painted here must not be overlooked. It does not merely explain why Hengest could not escape in his ship; it is also a symbol of the deep depression of his spirits, the lethargy of despair which extinguished all his native energy and enterprise. But that state of mind was not enduring. Hengest's mood changed with the turn of the year and the advent of spring. This being so it is not mere commonplace (as Boer has objected) when the poet tells us that winter lasted until the new year came, for the end of winter means the end of Hengest's cold fit. Bearing this in mind and also that the *wuldor-torhtan weder* (the sun-bright seasons) are an obvious antithesis to the *wæl-fagne winter* of l. 1128, I think the difficulties that have been raised as to the meaning of the above passage will disappear.

Obviously the new year brings the sun-bright seasons; I therefore take *weder* in apposition to *sele* and assume that the logically necessary expression for the recipient is left to be inferred as at l. 1428, *ða on undern-mæl oft bewitigað sorh-fulne sið on segl-rade* (*i.e.* sea-monsters which often provide an anxious journey for the mariner). Hence I translate "until another year came to the abodes of men (the personification is to be noted, cp. my remark above on *wæl-fag*) as they still do, (the years) which ever provide our happiness (happy time), the sun-lit seasons (*i.e.* spring and summer)." That an abstract noun may be varied by a concrete one—which relation I here assume between *sele* and *weder*—is of course well known[1]. It seems usual to take *weder* as in apposition with *gear*, *i.e.* as a sort of collective variant of that idea[2]. But this ignores the pregnant meaning of *wuldor-torhtan*, for the sun-lit seasons are at most the equivalent of half the year, not the whole. Probably the scribe who altered *doað* to *deð* made the same mistake. The change of number in *oþ ðæt oþer com gear...swa nu gyt doað*, is of course sufficiently attested by the metre; and is another example of the phenomenon to which I have already referred as almost regular in *Beowulf*[3].

---

[1] Cp. Klaeber, *Modern Philology*, III, 239.
[2] But cf. Heyne-Schücking, 12th ed., under *beweotian*.
[3] Cp. above, p. 49.

1137 *b*   fundode wrecca,
         gist of geardum;

I remark that *fundian* evidently means to be under a strong impulse to remove either, definitely, to a particular place, or, less definitely, from somewhere. In the context there is therefore a temptation to connect this statement with the former one: *eard gemunde*; and to understand that when the ice broke up on the sea Hengest felt impelled to take in earnest to his ship and sail forth, away from Friesland. The whole point of the situation is however made clear in what immediately follows. Not the sea-journey was now in Hengest's thoughts, but plans of revenge. Thoughts of escape were definitely dismissed from his mind. We must therefore understand *fundode* in its indefinite sense. The stranger (*gist*) at Finn's court, the lonely stranger (*wrecca* = exile), felt himself driven forth from the abodes of men (*of geardum*).

I consider, therefore, that we have here the expression of the restlessness which seized on Hengest when spring returned and which drove him forth from the hated society of the Frisians to commune in solitude with his own thoughts.

1140   gif he torn-gemot   þurhteon mihte,
         þæt he Eotena bearn   inne gemunde.

These lines afford a very good test of the two possible hypotheses as to who the Eotens are. It is noticeable that hardly any two adherents of the popular theory that the Eotens belong to the Frisian side have given the same explanation of these lines. It is indeed on this theory very difficult to make out whether the *þæt* is to be taken as a pronoun or a conjunction, since, taken either way, it gives a forced sense or compels us to emend. All these difficulties can be easily got rid of by assuming that the Eotens are Danes. This leaves us free to understand *bearn* as apposition to *he* whereby *þæt* falls easily into place as object of *gemunde*, and this verb can be taken in its literal sense, as also the infinitive *þurhteon* in the preceding line; *inne* remains the adverb we should expect it to be, with a meaning as in l. 2113, *hreðer inne weoll*. We arrive thus at the translation "whether he could carry through the fight, which he, the son of the Eotens, was inwardly recalling."

We have already seen that the fight in the hall had been left unfinished, and for the Danes in a highly unsatisfactory way, because their sovereign had fallen unavenged. It is implicit in ll. 1130–31 and again in ll. 1139–40 that Hengest had been thinking of escape and we now learn that under the reviving influence of spring his thoughts had taken quite another turn. No longer does he think of escape but of revenge. But such thoughts naturally call up to mind that unfinished fight in which his lord fell, and set him revolving plans to bring about a proper conclusion to it, *i.e.* by slaying Finn. The appositive *Eotena bearn* emphasizes his standpoint in the matter. As son of the Eotens he *must* recall the conflict (*torn-gemot* is comparable with *hond-gemot*). The *inne* reminds us that separated as he is from his followers he has no one near to whom he can confide his thoughts.

It speaks strongly for this interpretation, in my opinion, that we now have an obvious antithesis between *eard gemunde* and *torn-gemot gemunde*. The whole passage from l. 1127 *b* on has an antithetic structure evidently conveying the revolution in Hengest's mind. On the one hand we have the contrasted pictures of winter and spring; on the other the images, first, of Hengest lonely and dejected, then, of Hengest still isolated but full of reawakened energy. Parallel to the first we have the antithetic expressions *wæl-fagne winter* and *wuldor-torhtan weder*, to the second the expressions *eard gemunde* and *torn-gemot gemunde*, the opposition between thoughts of escape and plans of vengeance. There is a true opposition between the last-mentioned ideas. If Hengest were to flee, Finn's suspicions would be aroused, he would be on his guard.

> 1142   Swa he ne forwyrnde   worold-rædenne,
> þonne him Hunlafing   hilde-leoman,
> billa selest,   on bearm dyde;
> þæs wæron mid Eotenum   ecge cuðe.

The manifold differences in the interpretation of these lines arise mainly from the difficulty of finding a satisfactory sense for *worold-ræden* which occurs only here, coupled with the fact that the introductory particles *swa* and *þonne* are ambiguous in their function—they may, of course, be either adverbs or conjunctions—while in addition *lafing* is ambiguous in form and *Eotenum*, once more, ambiguous in its reference. It is very doubtful, however, whether there is any justification for boggling over *on bearm dyde*. *Don* of course has as one of its regular functions that of denoting purposive activity without reference to its special form, like Modern English "put." Consequently it may mean here either "lay" or "thrust," both of which have been suggested. On the other hand while *bearm*, as well as "lap" may have the meaning "breast," it does not have the latter meaning in the anatomical sense of the word; it does not denote a part of the human body. *Bearm* denotes either *sinus* or *gremium*, *i.e.* the hollow between the breasts, or that formed by the thighs of a sitting person. Consequently while we can translate "thrust the sword into his bosom," that cannot be taken in the sense of "pierced his breast with a sword"; it could only mean "laid the sword hastily or forcibly in his bosom." It seems to me, therefore, quite impossible to find here an indication that Hengest or anyone else was killed. The only meaning that is really justifiable is that a sword was handed to someone. As regards *worold-ræden*, there is little help to be found from its form on account of the unhappy ambiguity of *ræden*, which may be either a substantive with meanings ranging from "government" to "stipulation" (Sweet), or an abstract suffix with no definite shade of meaning. Under these circumstances the meaning of this compound form can only be found inductively with the aid of a hypothesis framed on our conception of the context so as to allow a possible relation between *worold* and *ræden* to be deduced from it.

We have just been told that with returning spring Hengest's thoughts turned to vengeance, and we therefore have a natural expectation to learn the result of his cogitations. Now the thoughts he harboured certainly imply a conflict in Hengest's mind, the conflict namely between remembrance of the pledges he had given to Finn and the awakened desire to revenge Hnæf. The upshot can only have been one of two things; either Hengest resolved to abide by his oath to his new lord and put aside his vengeful thoughts, or he gave in to these and made up his mind to break the allegiance which necessity had forced on him. Approaching l. 1142 from this standpoint, I remark first that there are good reasons for declining to take *swa* here as conjunction, and for believing that as adverb it introduces a consequence[1]. It therefore certainly harmonizes with the hypothesis that the subject is still Hengest and that in this sentence the poet tells us what came of his thinking. Now *he ne forwyrnde* can hardly imply mere passivity, the probability is that it implies active acceptance. What is that *worold-ræden* which Hengest on this assumption accepted? If we have seen correctly so far, it must be something that harmonizes with either Hengest's determination to remain loyal to his new lord or his decision not to be loyal in this sense. Can we decide between these alternatives?

It is noticeable that both these alternatives have a common feature. In either case it is a question of obligation. Hnæf's death left Hengest under an obligation to avenge him, which derived from the generally accepted opinion of his day that revenge was a holy duty for every man. This obligation was not removed but only suspended by the altogether exceptional necessity in which he found himself of giving pledges to Finn not to take revenge; it was suspended merely because—as noted above—in the situation of the moment he could not take revenge. Once, however, he had escaped from that situation by swearing fealty to Finn, revenge once more became a possibility, and the old obligation, for men of those

---

[1] The proof of this I had originally intended to give in an appendix, but as it involved me in an investigation of the whole question of the functions of *swa*, the result considerably exceeded the decent limits of an appendix to an essay. Hence I decided to reserve it for the present, and will take the first opportunity of publishing it elsewhere.

days doubtless the most generally binding of all obligations, therefore became binding again. Hengest must consequently have felt in his freer situation that he was twice bound, once by the duty to take revenge and once by the duty not to break his oath to Finn. Of these, however, the latter would doubtless appear to him as a special and isolated case only holding good as long as he was in the exceptional situation which made it necessary to swear allegiance against his instinct and his will. Once the exceptional necessity had lost its force this special case would for his feeling no longer have power to suspend the generally approved and accepted obligation of avenging one's friend. The poet dwells on Hengest's state of mind in a way which proves that it is connected with the final tragedy, the death of Finn at the end of the story. He is obviously leading up to this catastrophe, and it follows therefore that Hengest must have settled the conflict in his own mind between the two forms of obligation outlined above by accepting that one which had the most generally binding force, the duty of revenge.

Now *worold-ræden* cannot mean "duty of revenge," but if this duty were felt in those days as the most generally binding, the one ranking above all others, which is highly probable, at any rate as regards the relations between men in court and camp, it would be quite sufficient to refer to it as such because this could only imply one thing, revenge. The question therefore arises, can *worold-ræden* mean "the general obligation"?

The comparison with Gothic *(ga)raidjan, garaideins* suggests as the primary meaning of *ræden*, "prescription, rule." This is supported by *folc-ræden* = plebiscite, *i.e.* rule or ruling adopted by the people. It is not contradicted by the meanings of the simplex (as given by Sweet and Bosworth-Toller), for these, though not derivable from one another, could conceivably have split off from the above primary meaning. Now it is certainly possible that this primary meaning, or something near to it, might have survived in the *worold-ræden* of our text; which without doubt takes us back to an early period of the language. Furthermore, *worold-ræden* naturally associates itself with *folc-ræden*, since *worold* can certainly denote the more comprehensive idea of which the *folc* is a part, so that if *folc-ræden* denotes what is adopted by the people as their ruling, *worold-ræden* may very well denote what is accepted in the world by all peoples.

I therefore translate l. 1142, "So he did not seek to evade the universal obligation," and believe that with the context this would at once be understood by the hearer of those days as meaning that Hengest resolved to take revenge for his fallen lord.

We are now faced by the problem of deciding the function of *þonne* in l. 1143. There are two alternatives: either we are told that Hengest made up his mind *when* a sword was laid in his lap, or *þonne* denotes temporal succession[1], and we are told, he made up his mind and *then* someone laid a sword in his lap. The decision between these two is not helped by formal criteria; it can only be arrived at on grounds of interpretation.

The first of these alternatives would imply that some impetus from without brought the conflict in Hengest's mind to an end. The second would have no such clear connection with foregoing events. It would only introduce the picturesque detail that a famous sword was presented to Hengest, which became presumably the instrument of the death of Finn. The first alternative, again, would imply that the lonely Hengest found it difficult unaided to master the conflict in his mind and was glad to submit to an external influence on his decision. On the other hand, the second alternative would introduce a circumstance not vital to the story, which the poet, who is trying to compress, could easily have done without, for Finn's death does not necessarily hinge on Hengest's wielding a particular sword.

Þonne as conjunction gives us then a fine psychological trait which, if present to the poet's mind, no amount of haste could very well lead him to pass over; as adverb it presents

[1] Cp. Schücking, *Satzverknüpfung*, p. 121.

us only with a romantic feature at variance with his decided tendency to drop all unnecessary detail. There is little need to hesitate about which alternative is preferable, if it can be explained how the presentation of a sword could influence Hengest's decision.

We get a hint in *Hunlafing*. This is naturally a single word; for, although the termination *-ing may* be that of a patronymic or a sword-name (or for that matter a river-name), where there are no indications to the contrary, it must as a mere matter of statistics be taken as probably denoting a patronymic. And while there is no concurrent evidence of *Lafing* as a sword-name there is such to support *Hunlafing*, for the tradition of the *Skjoldungasaga* proves that a Hunlaf was later remembered as being closely related to both a Guthlaf and an Ordlaf, names which occur in the Fragment and must be equated with the Guthlaf and Oslaf of the Episode (l. 1149).

Arngrim's table shows us unexpectedly the family of the *Lafingas* adorning the genealogy of the Scylding dynasty. But in the Scandinavian sources[1] the lists of the early Danish kings have an obvious tendency to incorporate the names of those whom a wilting tradition brought in any way in contact with Scyld's descendants—even their enemies, *e.g.* the Heatho-Beardan, Froda and Ingeld. It can hardly therefore be fortuitous that the Guthlaf and Ordlaf (Oslaf) of the Anglo-Saxon poems correspond to Gunnleifus and Oddleifus, or that Guthlaf's son Gar(ulf) is paralleled by Geir(leifus). The Lafing family must have entered the genealogy because they were associated with the Scyldings in some way or another and this association may very well have come about through their lord *Hnæf Scyldinga*. Hnæf's name in this connection would easily be forgotten if once his chief claim to remembrance lay in his relations to the Frisian monarch, but the closely associated group of names in *-leif* would tend to persist.

We learn, therefore, that a son (or retainer) of Hunlaf laid a sword in the lap of Hengest. Now Guthlaf and Oslaf, as

[1] Cp. Müllenhoff, *Beovulf*, pp. 34 ff.

the Fragment shows, were present at the first fight in Finn's hall, and, as the Episode shows, they survived their monarch Hnæf. They must, therefore, have accompanied the rest of the Danes when after the treaty these were separated from Hengest and went to their quarters in the *hea-burh*. Since it was a Hunlafing who handed over the sword, it may be presumed that he came from the Lafing brothers as a messenger to Hengest at Finn's burg. Furthermore, since it would be difficult for the separated parties under the circumstances to communicate their secret thoughts to one another, this makes it seem likely that the laying of the sword in Hengest's lap was a symbolical act.

We must accordingly enquire whether we are told anything further about the sword which would illustrate its power of being a symbol easily understood by Hengest in the circumstances. This brings us to the consideration of l. 1145.

Those who consider the Eotens to be of the Frisian party see in this line an argument in support of their theory, and it will be well therefore to consider the relative value of the two hypotheses about the reference of the name in their bearing on the immediate question under discussion. It has been argued that it is more natural to ascribe knowledge of a famous sword to enemies than friends, especially when, as here, the edges of the sword are emphasized. Now the edges are of course symbolical of the death-dealing properties of the weapon, but it cannot really be asserted that the deadly effect produced by a sword in action would be less visible to friends than to foes. The question accordingly turns on, whether the poet is thinking of knowledge that is peculiar to certain individuals, *i.e.* those who felt the edges in the flesh (who would of course be enemies), or of knowledge that is common to a whole group of witnesses. That the latter is meant is clear from the mention of the clan name *Eotenum*. The sword is known because there have been numerous witnesses of the prowess of the owner among a whole clan (*mid Eotenum*), and as these witnesses might be either friends or foes the line is so far by itself quite inconclusive as to who the Eotens are. But must it remain equally inconclusive if we reason further? The usual construction of *cuð* is with the dative of the person to whom something is known. Now in Modern English there is a fine distinction between "known to" and "known among." If we say that something is known "among a man's friends," we imply that it is a matter of common knowledge gained from experience in a group of people who, as members of the group, have daily facilities of making some observation. If we say, however, that it is "known to his friends," we imply that it is known to individuals who as friends have any means of knowing. This shows it to be possible that there was a shade of difference between the two constructions of *cuð*, and, if so, it can hardly have been otherwise than that between "known to" and "among," between common knowledge and individual knowledge. Now the speaker is more likely to associate the idea of common knowledge of a man's belongings or attributes with the idea of the man's friends than with that of his foes, with the idea of his national than with that of a foreign group. This being so, there is something more than mere possibility, namely at least a shade of probability, that *mid Eotenum* in l. 1145 would refer rather to Hengest's people than to the Frisians.

From this we see that l. 1145 not merely does not prove that the Eotens are of the Frisian party, but that the chances are, if anything, against the hypothesis of their being so. The line, therefore, harmonizes with everything which I have previously argued in regard to the reference of this name to the people of Hnæf.

If we now ask what is implied by the laying on Hengest's lap of a sword which was a familiar object among the Eotens, I think it is evident that the implication is that the sword was well known to Hengest and immediately recognized by him: in other words, the sword reminded Hengest of its owner. We are therefore told in these lines that Hengest did something when he was reminded of someone, and that certainly permits the inference that he was reminded on purpose, that the presentation of the sword to him was intended to remind him of someone. Now of course many swords were recognizable by Hengest, but it cannot be the intention of the poet to tell us here that he was reminded of someone who was quite indifferent to the audience. The poet must have counted on his audience as well as Hengest being reminded of someone, a person whom he himself had in mind because of the rôle allotted to him in the story. He must have felt that when he referred to a sword which produced an immediate effect on Hengest's mind, everyone would immediately say to himself, Ha, so-and-so's sword! But who was so-and-so? There can only be one answer in the circumstances: Hnæf! The occasion, therefore, of Hengest's taking a certain action in consequence of all his previous cogitations about the possibility of revenge was his being reminded by someone else of Hnæf, and as this person reminded him through the symbol of a sword, that is a pretty sure hint that Hengest was to be reminded not merely of Hnæf but of the desirability of avenging him. Hengest, therefore, drew the consequence from his own imaginings when he discovered that the thoughts of others of his band were moving in the same direction, and this consequence was: "he did not reject the *worold-ræden*, the universal obligation."[1]

The situation then is as follows: To Hengest, undecided and lonely, tortured by memories of that unfinished fight in which his lord fell, comes a messenger from the *hea-burh* bearing a mute reminder of the dead[2]. That is decisive. He can no longer hang back now that he knows he is expected by others (who are equally bound with himself!) to shake off the unnatural fetters which not the normal order of things, but cruel and exceptional necessity, had forced on him.

---

[1] As I tried to show above, his problem was, which of two obligations he should reject.

[2] Cp. the rôle of the *gomelra laf* in the famous passage about the whetting of the Heathobeardan, ll. 2032 ff.

1146 Swylce ferhð-frecan   Fin eft begeat
      sweord-bealo sliðen   æt his selfes ham,
      siþðan grimne gripe   Guðlaf ond Oslaf
      æfter sæ-siðe   sorge mændon,
1150 ætwiton weana dæl;   ne meahte wæfre mod
      forhabban in hreþre.

Swylce I regard as meaning "in such wise," *i.e.* in the manner indicated by the foregoing, where we have learned that Hengest and the occupants of the *hea-burh* are at one in the desire for revenge[1]. I take *siþðan* as conjunction, since it can hardly refer to something which took place after Finn's death. As regards the ambiguity of *sæ-siðe* which might refer either to a journey from Friesland to Hnæf's country, or the reverse, I think we have a clue in the *sæ-lade* of l. 1139. The latter has an obvious reference to the return journey of the Danes to their land. It is unlikely that the poet so soon afterwards would use the synonym *sæ-sið* in the reverse sense, especially as we know from the Fragment that Guthlaf and Oslaf (Ordlaf) were present at the outbreak of fighting in Finn's burg, and there is no hint of their having gone home before this. Besides, under what circumstances can we imagine two of the Danes sorrowfully announcing or complaining about the past at the court of Finn, where all such references are banned by a solemn undertaking on both sides —and this as a preliminary to taking revenge? Is it really likely that the Danes denounced the treaty, and gave Finn warning of their intention? The simplest explanation is certainly that Guthlaf and Oslaf had been sent back to the homeland to report what had happened and gather reinforcements[2]. The Hengest who ratified the treaty is obviously not the sort of person who takes unnecessary risks, and the small band in the *hea-burh* watched, as it would be, by jealous eyes,

---

[1] The proof of this I had also to reserve for the present, as *swylce* and *swa* belong together. Cp. n. to p. 94.

[2] Even if this took place openly, as far as the going was concerned, Finn could scarcely object, since it would be due to the Hocingas as a friendly nation to let them have authentic news of what had happened. Cp. my reconstruction of the situation below (p. 128).

is not likely to have offered by itself and without assistance a very effective instrument of vengeance.

There can be no objection on the score of style to taking the final remark (1150 *b*–51 *a*) as referring to Finn. It is probably the common epigrammatic summing up of a situation: "His flickering spirit had no power to restrain itself in the body," *i.e.* Finn was *wæl-fus*, his hour was come. The reminder of Beowulf's *wæfre sefa* (l. 2420) contained in *wæfre mod* can hardly be accidental.

There are so many problems connected with the Finn Episode that one hesitates to add a further one to an already long list. Still even at the risk of appearing extravagant, I am compelled to raise the question whether the epithet *ferhð-frecan* in l. 1146 must necessarily be taken as accusative in agreement with *Fin*. It may, of course, be a mere ornamental epithet and as such applicable to any hero, but taken with the full strength of its meaning (*animosus*) it does not seem well motivated for a description of the Frisian king as he appears in the Episode. Besides, in this passage (ll. 1146 ff.) Finn plays a purely passive rôle. Now if I was right in arguing[1] that the style of the Episode is governed by a supreme law of economy so far at least as its narrative elements, as distinct from those which come under the head of "elegiac expansion," are concerned, then it must be regarded as an inconcinnity that at this point Finn should be referred to by an expression which is surely not elegiac in tone but quite the reverse. On the other hand *ferhð-frec* (or rather the substantive *ferhð-freca*?) is an obviously suitable expression to be used of Hengest.

Furthermore, interpreted in the usual manner, it is a matter for surprise that after all the talk about Hengest's change of mind there is no indication in the following résumé of events of his direct participation in what takes place. Yet we look naturally for an indication of his playing here again the rôle of leader, as he certainly did in the first fight.

I suggest, therefore, that *ferhð-frecan* should be taken as genitive dependent on *sweord-bealo*. The sword-bale which

[1] See above, p. 16 f.

again (*eft*) overtakes Finn in his own home is the sword-bale of the "bold-minded" Hengest. The man whom Finn could not overcome "at that meeting-place," who was the principal cause of the death of most of his thanes, was also the person to whom Finn's death was due.

> 1151 *b*   Þa wæs heal hroden
>   feonda feorum,   swilce Fin slægen,

In spite of the weight of authority which backs up the emendation of *hroden* to *roden*, I cannot bring myself to accept it. It is of course conceivable that *feorh*, "life," might develop the meaning "living body" and thence take the final step to "dead body," but where is the proof that this actually took place in Anglo-Saxon? Certainly it cannot be taken to be proved by l. 1210, *Gehwearf þa in Francna fæðm feorh cyninges, breost-gewædu ond se beah somod*. The poet has just been telling of Hygelac's last expedition against the Frisians, in which he carried off much treasure but *under rande gecranc*. He goes on to explain (1) that not the Frisians but the Franks were responsible for Hygelac's death; (2) that his booty was lost again. Now various idioms in which *feorh* occurs show that life was regarded as a possession, the same conception as underlies modern phrases like "to sell, give or lay down one's life" (cp. *feorh siellan, agiefan, alecgan*, etc.). It was natural enough for the poet, therefore, to remark that Hygelac's personal possessions, including his life, fell into the power of the Franks, or as he says, putting the most precious thing first, his life, his armour and the wonderful ring as well. To translate here *feorh* by "corpse" is unsuitable, for that would not bring out plainly that Hygelac was slain by the Franks.

There is therefore no proof that *feorh* ever meant "dead body." Indeed there is hardly more that it ever meant even "living body," since the only support that has been produced for this is a line in *Genesis* (l. 2065): *and feonda feorh feollon ðicce*. But even here a translation like "the living bodies of the enemy fell thickly" is not very convincing; it is no better than "the corpses of the enemy fell thickly."

And when we find that what is at first sight a very promising example, namely, *het he ofn onhætan to cwale cnihta feorum*[1], has been rejected because it corresponds to the Latin *vitis juvenum*, it does not give us much courage to build further on the *Genesis* example.

Under these circumstances it seems safer to explain *feonda feorh* on the basis of the usual meanings of *feorh*, which are "life, spirit (vita, anima), living being." In that case the *feonda* is probably merely a genitive of origin, denoting the class to whom the beings in question belong.

At first sight it would then appear that such a collocation as *feonda feorh* would mean nothing more than *fiend* by itself, but closer inspection will I think reveal a difference. The plural *fiend* is what Sievers[2] calls a "summativvorstellung," it expresses the totality made up by all individuals who for the time being are classified as enemies. *Feonda feorh* is likewise a "summativvorstellung," but it expresses less than *fiend*, namely, a number of individuals belonging to the enemy, forming a part of the whole enemy group. The line quoted above from *Genesis* means "The enemy's men fell thickly," *i.e.* "a large number of the enemy fell."[3] *Fiend feollon ðicce* would mean "the enemy fell thickly," and there would be the same disagreeable lack of harmony between sense and form of the original as we can feel in the translation, because "the enemy" really means "all the enemies," whereas "thickly" limits the falling to some of them.

Of course it can be argued *a priori* that "human beings of enemy origin" may logically mean a group as large as that of the enemy, and therefore express exactly the same idea. Language, however, although it makes distinctions is by no means bound to make them logically, and in practice I think

---

[1] *Daniel*, 226.   [2] *PBB*. xxix, 569.
[3] In the translation I have used the collective expression which is more common in the modern language than the summative one. But we likewise use the latter in conjunction with a possessive pronoun, and we could therefore translate, "a large number of their enemies fell."

it will be found that the group of such and such origin is usually accepted as smaller than the original group. "A number of citizens" obviously does not mean "all the citizens," although the latter can be expressed also as a number.

Now of course I am aware that in the modern language phrases like "The enemy fell thickly" are common enough, and I do not therefore wish to aver that it is compulsory to make the distinction to which I have directed attention above. All I wish to point out is that the distinction can be made, and actually is made when we say instead of the foregoing "Large numbers of the enemy fell." Nor do I assert that it was compulsory to make the distinction in Anglo-Saxon, of which language I confess to a very imperfect knowledge. All I wish to prove is, that even if, as I believe, *feorh* could not mean "body" or "corpse," it is still possible to discern motives for the use of *feonda feorh* in a sense distinct from that of *fiend*.

Even, however, if we admitted the suppositive meaning of *feorh*, it is doubtful if the emendation to *roden* gives a really satisfactory sense. I say that in spite of the "evident richtig" with which it was greeted by one of our foremost authorities. Clark Hall, following this emendation, translates, "Then was the hall reddened with the corpses of the foes." What foes? Obviously the foes of the owner of the hall, for we can hardly ascribe to the poet a desire thus to imply "The foes of the attackers." That is to say, the poet, whose whole attention is concentrated on the fate of Finn, is credited with a desire to bring out that there was on this occasion a great slaughter of the Danes who slew Finn. I do not believe it. I have more respect for the memory of Hengest, who I am sure, once he had cast aside his scruples, saw to it that the job was carried through neatly and effectively with the minimum of loss on his side. Finn was caught napping in the very hall, which, as Hengest himself had proved, was capable of being defended against greatly superior numbers, and Hengest had carefully prepared measures to prevent any contretemps for the attacking force such as he himself had occasioned to the Frisians.

Furthermore, a remark about the slaughter of Finn's own warriors—supposing the poet to have said "foes" when he really meant "defenders"—does not seem to me here to be very well placed. The poet has not displayed the least interest in Finn's warriors since he mentioned the death of their leaders at a point where it was unavoidably necessary. Hildeburh, Finn, then Hildeburh again, Hengest and once more Finn, these are the actors in his drama, and the crowd in the background are mere dummies, individualized by no single trait. The climax is reached with the death of Finn and the plundering of his treasures; what does this poet care how many more of the vulgus lost their insignificant lives in the crowning catastrophe? It is quite clear that the devastation of Finn's burg must have been fatal to many of them, why labour the point? There is no bereaved monarch left to bemoan them, no Etzel and Dietrich to weep over the charred remains.

But, though frankly I regret it, *hroden* really calls for the knife. This particular Homer may have nodded, but not over his rhymes. He was no more likely to have left *heal hroden* in the second half-line, than was—shall I say?—Graf Platen to have rhymed "neige" with "schmerzenreiche."

What we really look for here is, I think, some indication, however superficial, of the manner of the final attack. The poet with his *swa* and his *swylce* to open the preceding sentences has shown a distinct tendency to "motivate" at this point, and in l. 1152 he has another *swilce* which can hardly mean "likewise," since he is not interested, as we have seen, in the slaying of anyone but Finn. It must, therefore, mean "in such wise," *i.e.* in the manner indicated by the sentence under discussion.

In fear and trembling—for here, truly, the vestiges are terrifying—I consequently suggest *broden* as offering the minimum of change from what is actually transmitted to us in the text, and at the same time some opportunity of constructing suitable sense. The translation I would give is:

"Then was the hall wreathed with a living chain of enemies and in this way Finn slain."

From the sure meaning of *bregdan*, "to weave," to the meaning "wreathe, encircle"[1] does not seem *a priori* an impossible transition.

Of course I am aware of the difficulty of proving that the quite occasional and metaphorical use of the word *bregdan* which I have suggested here, is not only possible, which will hardly be denied, but likewise probable. The past participle *bro(g)den* is conventionally used to describe the result of technical processes applied to artificial products of human ingenuity, the weaving of the chain-corslet, the ornamentation of objects with extraneous materials. Between that and the general sense of "encircling, surrounding" which might be applied to any object, if occasion arose, there is indeed a considerable gap. From the conventional designation of an object as "braided with precious stones" to a "hall braided with enemies" is a rather considerable leap, when there are no parallels to prove its probability.

On the other hand it is clear that the meaning "weave" is a specialization of the ordinary meaning of the verb, explained by the ordinary meaning itself. *Bregdan* obviously denotes vibratory movement to begin with, and hence is applicable especially to movements of the hands, that, like wielding the sword or the actions of the weaver, suggest a vibratory form of movement. Once this concentration of the meaning, however, on purposive motions of the human frame is established, it is only a step to the generalization of purposive movement as its meaning, without particular reference to the form of movement. The past participle would then apply not merely to the state of an object resulting from the particular action, say of weaving, but to any analogous state produced by purposive action. I think this proves at any rate its suitability for a metaphorical use such as I have suggested. A parallel to this process by which the usual association of a

---

[1] Cp. *brogden byrne, Elene,* 257, and *beag brogden wundrum eorcnanstanum, Phoenix,* 602.

special form with an idea of movement may be exchanged for the association of purposiveness, is afforded us in such a phrase of Modern English as "to throw a garrison into a town." I admit that I am here postulating for the poet a somewhat violent *tour de force* in thus squeezing the last resource out of an expression not ordinarily so used—but the whole Episode is a *tour de force*! And after all, "a hall en-woven with living beings" is rather more satisfactory than "a hall reddened with living beings," especially when we are invited to suppose that the living beings were—dead!

CHAPTER THREE

TRANSLATION OF THE EPISODE

THERE was song and the jubilation of men assembled together in the presence of Healfdene's war-leader; the harp resounded and many a lay rang out; then Hrothgar's scop was called on to roll forth his tale of hall-play along the mead-benches.

With the sons of Finn, when sudden disaster o'ertook them, the hero of the Half-Danes, Hnæf, ally of the Scyldings, was fated to fall in the slaughter of the Frisians. Nor indeed did Hildeburh feel bound to praise the Eotens' loyalty; in time of peace she was deprived of her dear ones, of sons and brothers, at that shield-play; they fell at the stroke of fate, transfixed by the spear. That was a mournful lady. Not without reason did Hoc's daughter grieve at her destiny, when the morning came and she could see in the clear rays of the sun murder raging among her relatives. Where he formerly held the highest earthly bliss, battle carried off all of Finn's thanes excepting only a few, so that he could not at that meeting-place at all conclude the struggle with Hengest nor wrest by fighting the fatal heirloom from the king's thane; but he and his counsellors offered him terms, that they should hand over to him another dwelling with hall and throne, that they should have opportunity to dispose of one half of the treasure as against the son of the Eotens, and at sharing of gifts the son of Folcwalda should daily honour the Danes, load Hengest's followers with rings, with costly jewels of plated gold, just to the same extent as he was wont to encourage the Frisian kin in the mead-hall. Then on both sides they ratified a firm treaty of peace. Finn swore to Hengest by oaths in accordance with agreement, that he would honourably hold the heirloom of disaster, true to the decision of the councillors; that there no man by word or deed should break the treaty nor with evil intent should ever mention it, although being without a lord they were to follow their chieftain's slayer, since such was their necessity; if then one of the Frisians with perilous speech should call up vengeful passions, then the sword's edge should afterward be his portion.

The oath-taking was finished and the precious gold had been raised from the hoard. The best warrior of the War-Scyldings was ready for the funeral pile. At that pyre was clear to view the corslet steeped in blood, the gilded swine's head, the boar's image encased in iron, many a noble who had perished of his wounds. All of them had fallen in the fray. Then at Hnæf's pyre did Hildeburh command that her own son be committed to the fierce glow, the bodies set alight and consumed with fire. Recumbent on his breast the poor lady mourned, poured forth her plaint of woe. The warrior ascended. The greatest of funeral fires twisted its way up to the clouds, roared in front of the mound; heads melted; wounds opened their gates; then blood gushed forth before the loathly grip (of the flames) on the body. Fire, the greediest of spirits, swallowed up all those of both peoples whom war had torn away; their best strength was departed.

Then the friendless warriors betook them to their quarters, to see the Frisian land, their (new) dwellings and citadel. Hengest still stayed with Finn as agreed, throughout the stricken winter; he thought of home: that he might yet be able to steer his ring-prowed ship over the waters. The sea heaved with storms, fought with the winds; winter held the waves locked in icy fetters, until the new year came to the abodes of men, as still do the years that ever provide our term of bliss, the sun-bright seasons. Then was winter departed, and earth's bosom fair to view; the unhappy guest wandered forth from the dwellings of men; he thought rather of vengeance than of the sea-journey, whether he could finish the combat that he, the Eotens' son, was inwardly recalling. So he did not reject the universal obligation when the Hunlafing laid the battle-brand, the best of weapons, on his lap—that sword's edges were known among the Eotens! In such wise it came that the cruel sword-bale of the bold-minded hero again o'erwhelmed Finn in his own home, when Guthlaf and Oslaf after their sea-journey had sorrowfully reported the grim contest, and denounced their load of woes; the wavering spirit could not abide in the body. Then was the hall ringed in with the enemy's men and in this wise Finn slain, the King among his body-guard, and the Queen taken. The bow-men of the Scyldings bore to their ships the whole household gear of the mighty king, all they could find in Finn's dwelling of jewels and gems of art. They bore away on the sea-journey the noble lady to the Danes, brought her to her people.

CHAPTER FOUR

RECONSTRUCTION OF THE FINN SAGA

THE problem of reconstructing the Finn Saga may be likened to that of reconstructing the skeleton of a primeval animal from an incomplete collection of its bones. The latter problem can be solved by the scientist because he knows that the lost animal was an organism, which fact enables him to reason from the known to the unknown parts. If he can picture to himself the missing bones in such wise that the hypothetic parts fit in with the known parts so as to form a unity, in which every part is organically related to its neighbour and to the whole, he can consider the problem solved.

Now a saga is of course not a living organism, but it is a product of human life, *i.e.* of the organic activity of human beings. The productive activity of an organism must give rise to organized results, and in this sense, as the outcome of such activity, a saga must be organic, a derived organism if not a primary, living one. The missing parts of the Finn Saga must therefore be pictured in an organic relation to the known parts.

Mere invention will not help us far in the task. The problem is so complex that it is necessary to simplify it. The obvious way to do this is to compare the incompletely known Finn Saga with some completely known organism of the same class which bears a general resemblance to it, if such be available. If then in the incomplete saga, X, we find a part A which likewise exists in the complete saga, Y, compared with it, and if in the latter we find another part, B, organically related to A, but missing in X, there is a presumption that B was also present in X; and if this fills in a gap and is not contradicted by anything else in X, the presence of B in the latter may be considered as established.

The advantage of so proceeding is obvious. If we merely invented the missing link B we should have no test of its historical probability in combination with *A*. We must remember that general causes do not explain everything in an organism. The effects we see in it are the product of the narrowing-down of the field of causation through the characteristic reaction of the organism to general causes. Every organism has therefore, so to speak, its own characteristic limitation of general causal relations. We might imagine a dozen reasons why Hnæf should be slain at Finn's burg. The problem is to find the one cause whose operation is organic to the Finn Saga. We can only judge of that by considering the structure of a similar organism that is better known to us.

Fortunately we have in the story of the Burgundians, which forms the second part of the *Nibelungenlied*, a saga whose general resemblance to the Finn Saga, first noted by Mone, cannot be questioned. More fortunately still this tale is preserved to us in different versions belonging to different times. It may be likened therefore not merely to a single individual but to a succession of such connected with each other by lineal descent. It is a whole family displayed to us in individuals who represent different stages in the development of the species. We are consequently in a position to compare the Finn Saga not with a single like individual but with our general idea of a whole species.

The general resemblance of the Finn Saga to the saga of the Burgundians may be summed up as follows: Both are tales of vengeance set in the circumstances of like situations which are pregnant with like possibilities. Both show us the followers of one prince accompanying him at the court of another prince, his brother-in-law, and in strife with the latter. Both show us the stranger party besieged by the home party in the house of the latter and defending themselves successfully for days against the attacks of superior forces. Both show us a catastrophic slaughter inflicted on the home party, coupled with inability of the strangers to maintain themselves indefinitely. Both show us men wearying of the bloodshed and casting about for means to end it before it attains its climax. Both show us the sense of a fate implicit in the tragic situation, a fate which must run its course in spite of any efforts to stop the motion of the wheel.

This general resemblance is so typical that we may without hesitation assign the Finn Saga to the same species as the saga of the Burgundians. We might be tempted indeed to go further and assign to the Finn Saga an early place in the lineal descent of the other. This has been affirmed by Boer[1] on the basis of the resemblance above mentioned, and raises an important issue for the history of the Nibelungen Saga, but it is irrelevant here, where we are merely concerned with reconstructing the Finn Saga, since for this purpose the argument from analogy is quite sufficient.

This last statement may shock some of my readers, for the argument from analogy does not stand in high repute. But it has its uses. So long as we do not argue that A together with B in Y is proof of the coexistence of A and B in X, but regard it merely as the starting-point for an induction by hypothesis, no harm can be done and much good may be obtained. I wish to make a systematic use of the resemblance above noted, but I hope it will be understood that any suggestion taken from the *Nibelungenlied*, or elsewhere, is only regarded as hypothesis and claims no consideration except in so far as it satisfies the usual tests. The whole construction I give is also only a hypothesis, for which I claim no value except in so far as it allows us to deduce from it the text of the Finn Episode.

As we saw, the *Beowulf* poet plunges *in medias res* in dealing with the Episode. He starts the story at the point where fighting had already broken out. He gives no indication of what brought Hnæf to Finn's burg nor what led up to the quarrel. This is the first problem that awaits solution.

Now it is a standing feature of the Burgundian tale that Gunther and his men came to Etzel's court at Etzel's invitation. This trait stands obviously in an organic relation with

---

[1] *Zs. f. d. A.* XLVII, 152; cp. *Untersuchungen über den Ursprung und die Entwickelung der Nibelungensage*, II, 199.

the ensuing tragedy, the poignancy of which is deepened by the circumstance that it ensues from what is, on the surface at any rate, a friendly act of one side towards the other. It is clearly a good "try" to start by introducing this feature into the Finn Saga. I assume, therefore, as many have done before, that Hnæf came to Finn because the latter invited him. This is borne out by the interpretation I offered of *unsynnum*, if that be correct.

But in a story the act of a person has little value apart from its motive. The outward succession of events is only the sign of the inward concatenation of motives. It is not enough to provide the Finn Saga with an opening event, we must also find the underlying motive.

In sending the invitation Attila's wife is always concerned as well as her husband, naturally, because it goes to her brother, but the pair are likewise at cross purposes. A result of this is that the Burgundians know what to expect, for in the early version (*e.g. Atlakviða*) Guthrun warns them of Attila's traitorous intent, in the later version (*Nibelungenlied*), where Etzel is innocent of evil design, Kriemhild is a warning in herself. This relationship of husband and wife is not necessary; it is only an alternative to the two being in harmony with each other. It cannot therefore be organic in the sense that no representative of the species to which both sagas belong could be without it. Indeed it is significant that Guthrun's rôle flows from the conception of Attila's character and Kriemhild's rôle from the conjunction with the Sigfrid Saga. We have, therefore, no right to import into the Finn Saga, along with the invitation, the trait of disagreement between Finn and Hildeburh, unless something else in the source should call for it, and nothing else does. We must therefore find a motive for sending the invitation of such a nature that Hildeburh could approve of it. This raises at the outset a very serious difficulty, for the following reason.

Attila's traitorous design flows from cupidity. He covets the treasure of the Burgundians. We cannot drop this so easily as we dropped the conflict between him and Guthrun, because, as we have seen, a treasure plays a rôle in the Finn Episode and it is the object of Finn's desire. It is true the Nibelungs' hoard likewise appears in the High German version of the Burgundian Saga without having any such significance as in the Norse. It might be equally unimportant in the Finn Saga, *i.e.* it might have no necessary connection with the invitation. But on the principle of choosing the more difficult, not the easier task, when there is something to explain, we must assume that Finn's desire to wrest the treasure from Hengest is as significant as Attila's covetousness, and has therefore to be connected with the invitation. We must try consequently to combine two things, which do not at first sight easily go together—namely, Finn's invitation as a prelude to possessing himself of Hnæf's treasure, and Hildeburh's approval of his design.

In the *Atlakviða* the envoy's message to Gunnar is stated at length and has a content which in view of what follows has excited surprise. Attila not only invites Gunnar to visit him, but adds to the invitation promises of really royal munificence; the visitor is to receive weapons, horses, harness, broad lands and men. These promises cannot refer to the parting gifts which ancient custom prescribed to the host; they are something more, much more, namely the warlike outfit and the material rewards of effective service which the *beaggyfa* was wont to lavish on a distinguished retainer. It is plain, Attila's invitation is not merely one to pay a friendly visit, it is likewise an invitation to Gunnar to accept the host as his overlord.

Gunnar's response to the message—"I am just as rich and powerful as Attila"—shows that he understands what is implied, for it would be no reason for rejecting parting gifts from a host, if there were but a question of such. It can only mean, "I am Attila's equal in all respects and have consequently no grounds for seeking his protection."

The interesting story of Munderic in Gregory of Tours, to which I referred above, offers an interesting parallel. When Theuderic heard of his subject's rebellion, he sent a message to Munderic, to this effect: Accede ad me, et si tibi aliqua de dominatione regni nostri portio debetur, accipe. (This amounts to saying: Return to your allegiance, all will be forgiven, and you will receive your share of what is owing to a loyal vassal.) Dolose enim haec Theudericus dicebat, scilicet ut, cum ad eum venisset, interficeretur. Ille vero noluit, dicens: Ite, renuntiate regi vestro, quia rex sum sicut et ille. As in the *Atlakviða* we have the double-barrelled invitation: Come to me and be my vassal; and the single response: I am as good as your master.

Attila, though of course determined to stick at nothing, might be influenced by either of two alternative sets of motives. In the first place, if Gunnar were his undoubted equal, the invitation to declare himself a vassal, would be an insult and coupled with the invitation to come to Hunaland would be furthermore a challenge, which could hardly be rejected without an imputation of cowardice. In this case Attila's disloyalty would lie in breaking the peace between the related households, and his intention would be to force a conflict on terms favourable to himself. In the second place, if Gunnar were not Attila's equal but a monarch of much less potency, a quite different set of motives might have come into play. To bring this out clearly it will however be advisable to recall certain features of Teutonic life in court and camp.

The relationship between the Teutonic "ringspender" and the followers of high rank who lived at his court, enjoyed his protection, and fought his battles for him was a singularly intimate one, based on an extreme conception of loyalty. The retainer was expected to devote his whole personality to the service of his protector (in *Beowulf*, *hleo*), and in those days the idea of personality included everything that belonged to a man, not only what we call nowadays personal qualities but also personal effects. It was a common thing for the retainer to present to his lord his most valued possessions[1]. Of course such devotion could only be preserved in the rough

---

[1] Cp. Chadwick, *Origin of the English Nation*, p. 167.

and tumble of human affairs on a basis of mutuality. The chief was supposed to be generous and return with interest the attentions of his vassal[1]. All this is well exemplified in the relations of Hygelac and Beowulf[2]. No doubt Attila was bent on getting the treasure by foul means, if necessary; both Guthrun's warning to her brothers and his own character are a clear proof of this. On the other hand (it will be remembered that we are now supposing Gunnar not to have been his equal), he may have been quite willing to adopt gentle means if they were available, reserving treachery as a last resort. And apparently such means were available, because if he could induce Gunnar to become his vassal, the latter could hardly escape the obligation to show devotion by the sacrifice of property, *i.e.* Attila would have, if not a right to Gunnar's treasure, at least a claim guaranteed by custom; even as nowadays an accepted invitation to a wedding imposes a customary obligation to acknowledge it by a gift.

It is not easy to say whether either of these conceptions of the invitation predominates in the *Atlakviða*. The fact that Attila places guards against an attack by Gunnar and his men (St. xiv. 12)[3] which he obviously expects, speaks for a challenge. Gunnar's response to the message would be in place, whichever the conception, since it agrees with Munderic's, who was certainly not Theuderic's equal. On the other hand the circumstance that Gunnar does not attack Attila, but comes without any army to Hunaland, is against the challenge and for the second of the above alternatives. The reason of this may be that the author did not wish to admit that Gunnar was not Attila's equal, and consequently retained (or introduced?) a trait which showed the latter's nervousness consequent on his having issued a challenge; while, on the other hand, he did not like to lose the chance of displaying Gunnar's dare-devil courage, which followed from the second alternative view of Attila's superior might and importance, and the consequent motivation of the message.

---

[1] Chadwick, *loc. cit.* p. 168; Neckel, *PBB.* XLI, 424 f.
[2] Chambers, *Widsith*, p. 25.   [3] Neckel's edition.

However that may be, we have sufficient evidence to justify us in assuming that the double-barrelled invitation with either of the above sets of motives according to circumstances, is organic in the species to which the Finn Saga belongs. There can be no doubt, however, that only the second set of motives fits the Finn Saga, for Hnæf the dependent of the Scyldings cannot possibly be the equal in importance of Finn the great Frisian king, with a court which is obviously a centre of attraction. We must, however, drop the traitorous intent on Finn's part. It is not necessary, for a desire to obtain something by foul means is only an alternative to a desire to get it fairly; which is likely to be present depends on the character of the wisher. Finn's character is, however, quite different from Attila's. Finn has been washed clean by Chambers and I found in my examination of the text of the Episode no reason to besmirch his reputation again. There is nothing necessarily evil in Finn's desire to possess Hnæf's treasure. It is not covetous to desire my neighbour's field if I am willing to pay a fair price for it, and not wrong to try by fair means to induce him to part with it. The offer of a great monarch to take a lesser prince under his protection and increase his territory would, in the circumstances of those days, be fair dealing, even if intended to lead up to a transference of treasure, so long as there was no intention of the monarch to proceed treacherously. And the passive rôle of Hildeburh is altogether against treachery on Finn's side. She may well have wished that her brother should be Finn's vassal, increasing his own fame while he added to her husband's might.

It might perhaps be objected that if there were a question of transferring Hnæf's treasure, then the Scyldings, with whom he was already connected, would likely be in the field before Finn, and have at any rate a much superior claim to such transference. It is a fair objection but by no means insuperable. We noted before that Hnæf probably belonged at this time to the "auswärtige Gefolgschaft" of the Danes; as a member of the Scyldings' "ingesinde" he could scarcely be present, "on his own," as he obviously was, at Finn's burg. But the tie of the "auswärtiger Gefolgsmann" was undoubtedly less binding than that of the vassal who lived with his lord. It was probably a virtual independence, an easy alliance: earned and guaranteed by the former condition, which a man of high rank would exchange for the looser bonds, when he inherited from a father who had ruled over his own territory. We can conceive Hnæf as having served at the Danish court in his earlier days, and having left it rich in honours and rewards, to succeed his father in his native land. If the acquisition of the treasure then followed, Hnæf would have no particular motive for placing it at the disposal of the Scyldings and the latter would most likely have no such expectation. On the other hand, the family tie might easily be an excuse, coupled with Finn's superior might, for the latter to make proposals to Hnæf, which would be presumptuous in anyone else.

And we can hardly doubt that even backed by his honest intentions Finn's invitation was not usual, a divagation from the normal, not contradicted by the implications of custom indeed, but only weakly sanctioned by precedent. That a powerful monarch should tout for retainers was clearly nothing out of the common[1], but there would be the limitations of decency to observe. The pessimistic outlook, the dark cloud of premonition which hangs over the Burgundian Saga from the outset, are organic in the species. We are dealing with a fate-tragedy; the presence of the hoard, the symbol of good fortune hanging on the brink of disaster, is a sure sign. Finn was a personage of no small political talent, a master in the way of attaining his ends through negotiation, as the treaty he made with Hengest shows. He may well have trusted himself to gain Hnæf's treasure by negotiation and in a way quite honourable to both parties. The belief in the potency of face-to-face conversations is probably not entirely modern, for after all, it is based on human nature which is a fairly constant quantity. But an invitation is apt to be a

[1] Cp. *Beowulf*, ll. 2493 *b*–96.

double-edged tool. Come and talk matters over and settle things to the liking of both, is a request which can be interpreted in more than one way. Finn, conscious of rectitude, may have overlooked that. He shows something like overconfidence again in his dealings with Hengest. He was too sanguine.

I presume, therefore, that the invitation did not have precisely the effect that Finn anticipated: on Hnæf perhaps, who trusted others because he trusted himself. But the Finn Saga has room for the adviser who gives his vote against acceptance, as Hagen did in the *Nibelungenlied*. Someone will have noted the lack of precedent referred to above, and the conservative distrust of anything out of the ordinary will have aroused suspicion. Someone will have thought at once that Finn desired Hnæf's allegiance because he wanted his treasure, and that desires of this sort are dangerous because cupidity is a passion which cannot inspire confidence. To all representations of this sort Hnæf will have opposed his "Who's afraid?", and against the agreement of the brothers the voice of prudence will have been powerless. But suspicion once voiced is not easily allayed. Forebodings of misfortune will have darkened men's minds, and many will have felt, when the brothers set sail for Friesland, that they might never come back.

I picture to myself the subsequent course of events as follows: Hnæf and his men arrive in Friesland with a cloud hanging over them. The powerful adviser who had counselled refusal—let us call him Hengest, for there is a manifest parallelism between this character and Hagen—brought with him his gloomy distrust of the course events were taking, and communicated it to others. The nerves of the Hocings were on the strain, and they tried to balance their fears by an attitude of defiance. At Hengest's advice they refused to lay aside their arms when they entered the hall (as Beowulf does when he comes to Hrothgar, ll. 395–401, and as custom demanded). Finn, sanguine of being able to arrange matters, will have overlooked this, or pretended not to see it. After the ceremonious greetings were over, feasting began in the hall in celebration of the joyful reunion of the related royal personages. The guests sat down in full harness; the Frisians were *óbunir*[1]. Here we have a situation, in which obviously that puzzling *fær* which overtook the Frisians[2], might take place. On the one side unsuspecting hosts, overflowing with hospitality and unprepared for strife; on the other, the guests, armed, suspicious and resentful—only a spark is required to call forth a conflagration which will fall heavily on the entertainers. How came it about?

The *Þiðrikssaga* (cap. 406) affords a useful hint. During the feasting that was made for the Burgundians Grimhild calls her little son Aldrian to her side and bids him as a proof of his courage to slap Hogni's face. The boy does so and the insulted warrior hews him down with his sword, following this up by slaying the boy's tutor (who is thus made responsible for his pupil's bad manners). The same signal for the outbreak of hostilities in the hall occurs in the *Nibelungenlied*, with a different immediate motivation, namely, Dancwart's arrival with news of the massacre of the Burgundian men-at-arms in the *herberge*. In the one case Grimhild's display of spite is a devilish wile to place the onus on the Burgundians; in the other, Hagen's beginning on a defenceless boy is an outburst of savagery; in both cases Grimhild is the really responsible agent, *i.e.* the chain of causation runs between her and Hagen and links on to the Sigfrid Saga, with which this later edition of the Burgundian Saga is welded together.

The irresponsible act of a boy might shake the foundations of an empire, and Aldrian's behaviour does not necessarily require the instigation of a parent; the exuberance of youth would be a sufficient explanation. But we must be careful. One boy in a hall full of warriors is not likely to be feeling otherwise than shy. He would require some backing before his natural frivolity would well to the surface. I assume, therefore, the following:

---

[1] Cp. *Atlamal*, Str. 43 (Neckel). [2] *Beowulf*, l. 1068.

Finn had at least two sons, one a young man and the other a mere boy. The first egged the second—youth's love of practical joking and the arrogance of high birth combining to give confidence—to play a trick on one of the Danes. The stiff strangers who defied etiquette and sat down to the feast in their fighting gear, would be a challenge to wanton spirits, prone to seek the ridiculous side of things, and to find it in any departure from the normal. Hengest most likely would be singled out for their attentions, and Hengest reacted as Hagen did on a similar occasion. No one pays any attention to the whispering of the boys—and then suddenly, without warning, the headless corpse of Finn's son lies bleeding before the horror-struck spectators.

In a flash Hengest realizes that the moment he had dreaded is come. He sees red and a wild rage against the strangers who had entrapped him and his monarch, masters him. Before the hosts can grasp what is upon them he has dashed to the door of the hall, pitilessly hewing down anyone who seeks to bar his progress, and has cut off the escape of the unarmed Frisians. His mad excitement communicates itself in a flash to his fellows. All spring from their seats and draw their swords, and every Frisian who automatically makes to fetch his weapons is despatched on the spot. For the moment Hengest's volcanic outburst has completely turned the tables. The mighty Finn, surrounded by the flower of his warriors, is held in his own hall, like a rat in a trap; the small band of guests are masters of the situation.

Though aghast at what has happened Hnæf and his brothers have not lost their heads, like their followers[1]. There is no time to think out the consequences, but Hnæf realizes that Finn and Hildeburh bear no responsibility for the insult which Hengest has already wiped out in blood. The guest and brother is still held by the obligations of *sibb* and he responds nobly to the call, conscious only of the dominating impulse to protect his sister and brother-in-law against the unreasoning violence of his retainer. Whatever the future

[1] *Nibelungenlied*, 1967.

may bring forth, the responsibility for further bloodshed must not rest on the Danes. Finn and his queen must be permitted to leave the hall unharmed. And so it happens. Probably such of the Frisians as had not offered resistance are permitted to accompany their lord.

The Danes remain behind in the hall which has so dramatically passed into their possession. What will ensue is scarcely doubtful. The decision rests with Finn, who might perhaps be brought to patch up a reconciliation, but the Danes do not count on that[1]. Finn has his son (or sons) to avenge. He will hardly regard this as a personal matter between himself and Hengest, but is more likely to place a collective responsibility on Hnæf and his band of followers. So the Danes prepare for the worst. It need hardly be remarked that there is no thought of handing over Hengest to answer to Finn for his ruthless deed. From a modern standpoint Hengest is guilty of murder. No thought of crime would cross the minds of his companions. It would hardly even enter their heads to blame him for landing them through his lack of self-restraint in a desperate situation. Hnæf is Hengest's *hleo*, not his judge.

We now reach the situation with which the Fragment opens. Night has fallen. In expectation of an attack the Danes place guards at the door and lay themselves to sleep that they may keep fresh for the struggle. The expectation is not disappointed. Finn hastily brings together all the troops at his disposal and doubtless despatches messengers to beat the land to arms. By the light probably of fires kindled in the neighbourhood of the hall, fitfully aided by the rays of a watery moon, the onslaught begins[2].

In those days any building was a fortress easily defended by resolute men against a storm even in great force. The hall (the *hea-burh*) was probably the last refuge, which held out long after the outer ring of ditch and palisade had been taken. For merely defensive purposes the Danes were well placed. The fewness of their numbers would not make itself felt so

---

[1] Cp. Fragment, the speech of the *heaðo-geong cyning*, l. 3 f.
[2] Cp. the Fragment.

long as they were not forced into the open. In real life fatigue and starvation would be the chief danger. These seem to have been ignored by the poets, though the Burgundians penned in the burning hall at Etzel's court quench their thirst in blood. From drinking blood to eating human flesh is but a step!

Besides, the Danes have Hengest, whose character may be drawn with traits borrowed from Hagen—Hengest, the pessimist, who knows the joy of life only when at grips with death, whose iron soul fuses into glowing steel at the hot breath of mortal danger. A truly brilliant motif emerges now out of the welter of tragic forces: the struggle between Hengest, the man of character, and Finn, the man of brains, the nimble artist who has yet to learn (from Hengest) that human nature is not clay in his hands. Hnæf, the optimist, recedes into the background; the iron wheel of fate passes over him, for his mantle has already descended on the shoulders of his thane.

The Fragment breaks off tantalizingly in the middle of a question addressed by Finn to one of his warriors retiring wounded and disconsolate from the fray. Which of the two youths? he asks, and the rest is silence, for accident has withheld the answer from us. But one feels it to be: Hengest! Finn had good reason to ask why, after five days' ceaseless storm, the invincible garrison still held out, careless of their wounds. And now he learns clearly for the first time, what he is up against—the spirit and example of Hengest. That it is which animates and sustains the Danes, which nerves their failing muscles anew and teaches them to hug the spectre of sudden and painful dissolution with the exaltation of a lover.

Finn sets his teeth and lets the battle rage on, for every chord of his nature demands atonement for the slaughter of his sons; while the tough persistence of his political temperament keeps his original end in view. At last one of his objects is accomplished—atonement is exacted, for Hnæf and his brothers are fallen. The political side of him resumes the upper hand. A student of men, he has learnt to know the

greatness of Hengest and he acknowledges himself beaten
on þæm meðelstede—by Hengest. He will try him on another
field where he does not fear any superior.

We may understand this situation if we reflect that a fight
is not merely a test of physical but also of moral superiority.
A decisive victory can only be won by the side which shows
its moral superiority, and a victory gained by mere physical
strength is not decisive if the will to resist on the other side
has not been destroyed. The onslaught in which Hnæf fell
was doubtless intended by Finn as a crowning effort which
should finally smash both the physical and moral strength of
the garrison. It came near to success in leading to the death
of Hnæf, but Hengest survived and even the fall of his
chieftain could not bring him to acknowledge defeat. The
attack is bloodily repelled. After this the physical superiority
is still with Finn, but he knows now finally that a decisive
victory cannot be won by him over Hengest. In other words,
Finn feels Hengest's clearly established moral superiority as
a physical one, and gives up the thought of fighting further.

What follows, the treaty-making, the handing over of the
treasure, the funeral rites, the seclusion of the Danes as vassals
of Finn in a remote fortress and their separation from their
leader, is, I opine, clear enough from the text. Reconstruction
is here hardly necessary. Recapitulation will do. I have chosen
however to make Hengest the peace-breaker, who brought on
hostilities in a scene of rejoicing. This was not absolutely
necessary, for any other of the Danish notables would have
done as well, so far as the consequences are concerned; but
the rôle of Hagen in the nearly allied Burgundian Saga
certainly suggested Hengest rather than others. Now that
we have reached the treaty the objection may be raised that
Finn would not be likely to take the murderer of his own son
into his service. It is an obvious objection from the standpoint of modern feeling. It must be remembered, however,
that Finn could not regard Hengest as a criminal any more
than the latter's friends did. Hengest as an individual was
the avenger of his own honour, for he had been insulted. As

a Dane he was a breaker of the *sibb* and the slayer of the king's son; hence the Danes as a body owed atonement to Finn. Once, however, the atonement had been paid through Hnæf's death, Finn would have no technical claim against Hengest, and no objective grounds to treat him otherwise than the rest of the Danes; for just as *he* ranks as Hnæf's *bana*, so Hnæf would be the *bana* of his son. I do not argue that Finn would feel no further personal resentment against Hengest, but having once made up his mind to treat with the Danes he could only do so on the basis of neglecting such personal motives, and arranging matters with Hengest as the Danish leader, not as the agent of his son's death. So much self-restraint would be hardly possible if he did not have in the fall of Hnæf at least technical grounds for putting his feelings aside. Besides, there was mutuality in the proceeding. If he was overlooking Hengest's blood-guilt, Hengest on his side was expected to overlook Finn's rôle as the *bana* of his *beag-gyfa*. I think, therefore, that the objection to assuming Hengest as the peace-breaker instead of another Dane can be disregarded.

The treaty made between the parties reflects both the moral superiority of the Danes and the physical of the Frisians. From the first flows the guarantee of the Danes' security, contained in granting them another hall for the one they have so ably defended, as well as the arrangement that they are to retain half disposal (not possession) of the treasure. From the second, renunciation of their right to avenge their dead lord, the oath of fealty to Finn, and the transference of the treasure to their new protector. The common celebration of the funeral rites for the fallen seals the bond. The Danes then retire to the fortress allotted them as their future quarters, leaving Hengest to represent them at the court of Finn, who resumes the sway over his own residence, which had been so tragically interrupted.

In the winter months that follow there is little coming and going between the Danish quarters and the king's court. The humiliated survivors of Hnæf's band, dreading the Frisian arrogance, have little reason to seek the society of their new allies; they shut themselves off from the outer world. Finn, who has sworn to prevent them from being insulted, is content that there should be as little opportunity of friction as possible, and since he has Hengest in his immediate neighbourhood as a hostage for their good behaviour, has no objection to leave the Danes to their own devices. Hengest, therefore, is isolated among strangers. Lonely and homesick, his active mind frets itself into despondency when winter's storms and an ice-bound ocean cut him off from the only avenue of escape, by ship. But spring returns and the enterprising spirit of the man reasserts itself. As he wanders by the sea-shore his dreams of the far-away *eard* give way to memories of the fight in the hall; he remembers how the Danes flung back onslaught after onslaught and asserted their superiority in battle in the teeth of overwhelming odds. And then in the supreme moment the fight had to be broken off, because the Frisians acknowledged defeat, yes, defeat, and had recourse to negotiation! What followed? The humiliating oath which stern necessity exacted from the Danes, the oath to forget the slaying of their king and the holy duty of revenge. It is maddening! But Hengest is not the man to relapse into madness. While Hengest or a Dane lives, plans can be forged for vengeance. If only he had his men around him, to fire them anew with the spirit of their leader! Musing thus he returns to the castle and there the messenger awaits him with the well-known sword, Hnæf's sword, mute signal of the thoughts which the Danes are prevented from expressing otherwise in a place where their every action is spied upon. But now Hengest knows. His men have not forgotten, any more than he has. He can proceed tranquilly with his plans, sure of their co-operation.

How Hengest forged his opportunity does not appear clearly in the Episode. There is a hint, the sea-journey of Guthlaf and Oslaf, but it is difficult to unravel and has been variously understood. I attempt the following in reliance on my view of Finn's character.

Finn has his plans also. He is not the man to rest upon his oars nor let occasion slip by him. His design has been fulfilled, though not as he had expected or planned. Hnæf's treasure is in his hands, nor is he accountable for the disaster that placed it there. But cannot even thus much be turned into more? Hnæf is gone; his people deprived of their protector. Whither shall they turn for shelter? Why not to him? Are not the pick of the Half-Danes' notables already attached to his allegiance? Why should their country not follow them? It is a tempting idea to use those, who have already sworn fealty to him, to bring the rest of the shepherd-less people under his sway. In this way the exiles might unite with their own folk again, and Finn's kingdom be extended. There is no harm trying. So Finn proceeds to sound Hengest. And Hengest shows a laudable zeal to further the project. Soon it is arranged. Envoys are to be sent to Hnæf's homeland to explain the situation, and show that in the altered circumstances the future of the country must be sought in the protection of the Frisian king. What has happened is regrettable, disastrous. No one regrets it more than Finn, but one must face the logic of facts. These envoys must of course be picked among the Danes, and Guthlaf and Oslaf are selected. So they set forth ostensibly to do the bidding of Finn—in reality of Hengest.

Finn's plan is Hengest's opportunity. Acting on his instructions the envoys arrange when they arrive that reinforcements are to be sent secretly to land on the Frisian coast. The design is carried out successfully in accordance with Hengest's directions. One night while the Frisian king and his men are sleeping, the burg is surrounded by the new arrivals, led by Guthlaf and Oslaf. Hengest is awake to let them in—and the rest is simple.

CHAPTER FIVE

THE EPISODE AS INTERLUDE AND ITS COMPOSITION

UNDOUBTEDLY, as I remarked before, there is a parallel between Finn's burg and Heorot. Each of these places was a focus of national life and at each the fate of a people was decided by "hall-play," by mortal strife within the *hleo-burg*, by the shedding of blood in scenes dedicated to *worolde wyn*, to social enjoyment and revelry. But there is also a parallel within the parallel. Beowulf's exploit in defending Heorot against the attacks of a hitherto invincible monster can be compared with the great fight put up by Hengest and his associates against overwhelming odds.

Now I have claimed that the men of Hrothgar when they called on the scop for a tale of hall-play were thinking of Beowulf's *mærðo*; it had become an imperious necessity for them to assign their deliverer a place in the roll of fame amid the heroes of renown who had gone forth in search of adventure and triumphed over unheard-of difficulties. Some of these had distinguished themselves in hall-play—the question was, Had any of them performed an exploit of this kind equal to Beowulf's? And this question the scop was expected to answer.

If this be so, what the scop's auditors looked forward to was an inspiring description of deeds of skill and daring, of hand-to-hand encounters breathing the physical exaltation of desperate strife. And this is noticeably absent in the Episode; the deeds of the fighters whose prowess might have been compared with Beowulf's are barely alluded to, we are not even told that any champion conspicuously distinguished himself.

It follows, therefore, if the scop told the story as it is reported in the Episode, that either he wilfully disregarded the request of his audience, or I have misunderstood what his hearers wanted. Yet the indications are very plain that Beowulf's personality had captivated the imagination of the Danes, that all they thought of and spoke about was only what had reference direct or indirect to the hero of the hour. The scop who put them off with a parallel (and a gloomy one at that) between Heorot and Finn's burg, when he might have drawn a parallel between the fight in Heorot and the fight in Finn's burg, was a bungler. Either that, or the poet has not told us the same story as the scop told!

It is safe to assume that the scop was not a bungler. Like his fellows he was an admirer of Beowulf's and he was only waiting for the moment to come when the whole hall would hang on his lips as he declaimed his song of praise.

The question therefore arises: Had the poet of *Beowulf* at this point both a reason and an opportunity to substitute for the song of the scop something different, but not too different, something which would be superficially at least in harmony with the night of celebration in Heorot, that he was describing, and would at the same time serve an ulterior end of his own?

There can be little doubt about the opportunity. The fight at Finn's burg, the parallel to Beowulf's fight in Heorot, was contained in a wider complex, the Finn Saga.

To substitute the whole for the part was a little bit of sleight of hand which might easily escape detection, and it would be a temptation if the whole afforded a parallel which was of more importance to the author of the epic than the parallel which, we must assume, could only have been the aim of the scop. As the poet pictured to himself the revels of that evening in Heorot he must have heard his scop recite a tale, that, if it dealt with the Finn Saga at all, almost certainly had a great resemblance to the lay of which only a remnant is left to us in the Finnsburg Fragment. Now it is of course fairly clear that that lay did not contain the whole of the Finn Saga[1]; it dealt, like many other things of the same sort, only with one great and moving episode, namely,

[1] Cp. Ker, *Epic and Romance*, p. 84.

the *Freswæl*, the slaughter of the Frisians in the hall of their chieftain by a small and devoted band who had been penned in and surrounded. If the poet had set himself to report this lay as his scop recited it, he could not possibly have given us the Episode. Had he any reason to exchange it for another one of related content, one that dealt with the Finn Saga as a whole?

No doubt our epic suffers from "this radical defect, a disproportion that puts the irrelevances in the centre and the serious things on the outer edges"—only it should be remembered that what seems irrelevant to-day was not so yesterday, and that this Anglo-Saxon knight *sans peur et sans reproche* was born to triumph by God's help over the demons of darkness and to die with words of praise on his lips because he had won great treasure for his people—but there is nothing ragged about these outer edges. The picture is rounded off and complete. The hero performs his feats in a sun-lit foreground which stands out boldly against a background darkened by national, or, what in those days was the same thing, dynastic tragedy; and it is hardly saying too much to affirm that this background is for the poet of equal importance with the foreground. He has not merely the career and fate of his hero in view but also the career and fate of that hero's nation, the Geats, and of the nation with whom they were on friendly terms, the Danes. Little by little, taking advantage of every recurrent opportunity, he constructs his picture, allusively, it is true, but none the less unmistakably for his contemporaries, of the rise and fall of the two nations between whom Beowulf is a connecting link. Now it is a retrospect that reaches back behind the real events of his narrative, then it is premonition of approaching disaster that casts its shadow athwart the canvas. He cannot tell us of the building of Heorot without alluding to the flames which were finally to consume it, although they have no place in his plot. And this prescience which was really his own and his auditors' he projects into his characters. Wealhtheow dreads the family dissensions which are doomed to undermine the fortunes of the Scyldings and seeks to conciliate fate in the person of Hrothulf. Hrothgar preaches a long sermon to Beowulf on the vanity of human wishes. Beowulf concludes his recital of adventure on his return to Hygelac's court with a prophecy of impending strife between the Heatho-Beardan and the Scyldings, and when he himself dies the messenger who bears the tale foretells destruction to the Geats.

It is fairly plain that the poet and the people for whom he composed his epic treasured in a retentive memory the old homeland whence they had come across the sea to Britain, that from recollections of men and events in another clime and a former age they still drew their ideals of conduct, their conception of heroism. The kings, warriors, and clans of oral tradition stood in their eyes for a heroic age localized beyond the seas and in the past. But about this past they had no illusions. It was gone, never to return. Not merely were the heroes dead, but the peoples from whom they sprang had lived, had flourished and *wæs hira blæd scacen*. Nothing remained but the memory of their vicissitudes, the tragical interest of their fall, and the inspiring reminder that they had gone down fighting, unconquerable to the end. Looking back on these things it must have been difficult to view any episode however glorious without being reminded of a later one which formed a melancholy contrast; much as the modern student, when he conjures up a vision of Rome at the height of her power, can hardly avoid the thought of her decline and fall.

The poet knew what Hrothgar's scop could not know, that the parallel between Beowulf's fight with Grendel and the exploit of the Half-Danes in Finn's burg was contained in the wider parallel between the fate of Finn and the fate of the Scyldings. He knew that the latter were to fall in a final catastrophe that overtook Heorot[1], just as Finn in his last fight had perished in his own hall amid his own retainers. He who later on uses Beowulf as his mouthpiece to remind his

---

[1] Müllenhoff's contrary inference *ex silentio* (*Beovulf*, p. 47) is unnecessary; and indeed unlikely, in view of the hint in ll. 1164–65.

own audience of what the future held for Hrothgar and Freawaru may very well have felt that the lay of the scop was an opportunity to develop a parallel which would be plain to his hearers. Finn's catastrophe might have been a warning to Hrothgar's Danes if they had been able to lay it to heart, but, however it might have been with the Danes (and elated as they were by the turn of events they must in reality have been little prepared to take a gloomy view of the future), the warning would be something more to the listeners whose attention was fixed on one of the many oft-told stories of Heorot—it would be a prophecy. After this digression the poet's audience would feel more acutely the apprehensive tone which sounds through the further description of the night's doings in Heorot, the true inwardness of such remarks as that about Hrothgar and his nephew Hrothulf: *þa gyt wæs hiera sib ætgædere*, the pathos of the gentle Wealhtheow's appeal to her husband's kinsman, which reads almost like an entreaty that she might be spared the lot of Hildeburh.

In these circumstances the aim of the poet must have been not so much to tell the story of the Finn Saga as to recall the tragedy of it all, its bitter inevitability, to those who knew it well. And this he would best accomplish by showing how good men and true could be enveloped in misfortune without any real fault of their own. The accent, therefore, would lie on the situation and the characters—to display this situation in all its ghastliness and to indicate how heroic minds reacted to it would be the governing principle of his recital. Narrative would be relegated to the background.

It is possible that oral tradition favoured the poet. As well as ballads of the Fragment type dealing with the *Freswæl* there might be another whose main theme would be the sequel, and which, because some introductory recapitulation would be necessary, would in fact deal with the whole Saga. Nor would a ballad of the latter type necessarily be a long one. In it Hnæf might have had as little to do as in the Episode, and, as there, Finn and Hengest might bestride the stage. Such a ballad may very well have been in its skeleton actually coincident with the Episode. But even supposing this most favourable case, a ballad with such a disposition of the matter that it needed only to be reproduced in its framework in order to fit into the epic as an interlude serving the purposes required, even supposing this, it would only mean that the poet had wit enough to take his materials where he found them in a form suitable to his design and the internal economy of his poem. Whether he reduced the Saga by his own independent effort to the dimensions required or whether such a reduction was foreshadowed in the work of another, which only needed to be paraphrased, the Episode is worth analyzing with a view to testing whether its composition presents a possible grouping of the characters and incidents of the Saga as I have reconstructed it. Various features of such an analysis have already been employed inductively at different points in the process of interpretation and reconstruction. Such inductive use of these features implies the assumption that they could be deduced from the organism which was to be built up, and although it will entail repetition this assumption must now be put to trial.

The Episode presents to us a series of allusively drawn dramatic pictures, not stable like a painting, but full of vague movement like that of an imperfectly seen cinema show. To each successive picture unity is given by the light thrown on a single figure which focuses our attention and stands out against the perspective of shifting surroundings[1]. Thus, after an introductory remark we see first of all Hildeburh as the grief-stricken spectator of murderous strife among her relatives. Then we behold Finn with his advisers, offering terms of peace to the war-worn but defiant defenders of the hall. This picture merges into another of Finn publicly swearing the oaths by which he ratifies the treaty. The scene changes and against the background of the blazing pyre Hildeburh commits the body of her son to the flames. The

---

[1] The symmetrical arrangement of these pictures should be noticed. It may be symbolized by the central figures, thus: Hildeburh, Finn, Hildeburh, Hengest, Finn and Hildeburh.

first act is over and a transitional remark introduces the lonely and despairing Hengest confronted by the wintry, ice-bound sea that checkmates his longing to escape. This gives place to the laughing landscape of spring with the same central figure, brooding now on thoughts of revenge. A final picture shows the messenger from the *hea-burh* presenting Hnæf's sword to Hengest; then with a few swift crowded sentences of narrative the spectacle of Finn's burg melts away in ruin and hurried desertion of the stricken scene.

Thus we see it all in dumb show. Everything is described from the standpoint of one actor at a time. There is no dialogue, a sure sign that the Episode is not a lay in itself but only the précis of one.

The poignancy of the tragedy lies in the fact that against his will Finn set an avalanche rolling which first overwhelmed his brother-in-law and then in spite of all his efforts to restore the stability of things drew his own ruin after it. From this point of view Hnæf's heroic exit in a blaze of glory is of minor importance, mentioned curtly at the beginning as something bound to happen; it is the repercussion of his fall upon his *bana* which is a drastic example of the inexorableness of fate.

If I have come anywhere near the truth in my reconstruction of the Saga, the moving causes of the tragic conflict are given with the characters of Finn and Hengest. On the one hand the honest but ambitious Finn, ever seeking for means to extend his power and eager to add to his comitatus new recruits from amongst the most distinguished warriors of the day; on the other the dour and faithful thane, jealous of his chieftain's honour and reputation and quick to resent anything which looked like an attempt to take advantage of his lord's frank and trusting disposition. Finn knew well enough what he was about when he held out a friendly, though patronizing, hand to Hnæf, but there was an error in his calculations, for he had not reckoned with Hengest. With Hnæf he could easily have arranged matters, but the jealous, suspicious and defiant nature of the thane was a source from which tragedy was bound to spring.

The crisis of the drama is only reached when Finn and Hengest are brought face to face with none to intervene between them. Much must indeed happen before that takes place: Hnæf's journey accompanied by his unwilling but loyal and devoted follower, the accident which leads to a breach of the *sibb* that none could foresee, and the fatal consequences for both parties, the deaths of Finn's sons and the flower of his nobility, of Hnæf and his brothers. But all these predisposing events were well known to the poet's audience, as indeed was the whole story with its bitter ending. The economy of the epic called for a tragic interlude which would be in contrast with the careless revelry of the Danes freed from the incubus which had so long oppressed them, one which would illustrate the dark truth writ large across the memories of a dead and gone past: "There is no armour against Fate, Death lays his icy hand on Kings."[1] To drive this illustration home in the minds of his audience it was only necessary for the poet to confront Finn with Hengest amid the grim possibilities of the well-known situation, shortly to recall what that situation was in its naked horror, and recapitulate what Finn did and what Hengest felt under these circumstances. Finn true to himself as maker of the treaty, Hengest with equal inevitability driven to be its breaker— these were the dramatic figures which needed only to be presented with the appropriate staging.

Everything which happened in the Finn Saga, as I have reconstructed it, might have happened if Finn had been a widower, since Hildeburh's only importance is as a link between Finn and his brother-in-law. An abstract could easily be made without mentioning Hildeburh and without thereby leaving out anything essential to the narrative. It may seem, therefore, surprising that Hildeburh should receive so much attention in the Episode. The explanation has already been indicated. The poet was not, properly speaking, concerned with narrating what was already fully known, but with

---

[1] Cp. the comment at the conclusion of this episode in *Heorot*, ll. 1233 *b*– 35 *a*.

painting situations in which well-known events of tragic import were inevitable. The scene of desolation at Finn's burg after Hnæf's fall could not be more impressively brought out than by depicting its effect on Hildeburh, who without influence on the events stood between both parties and suffered on both sides. It is not her innocence which is so pathetic, for all are innocent of evil intention: it is her helplessness. Finn can labour to save what is to be saved from the ruin. Hengest can live on to fight again. For Hildeburh there is only one dramatic gesture left, the laying of her son's corpse on the pyre beside the uncle who had died in assuming responsibility for his murder—an action symbolic to the poet's hearers of the *sibb* which had been shattered indeed but never broken. And then, when the end comes, she is led back to her native land whence she had gone forth to become the queen of a great monarch—*sans* husband, *sans* children, *sans* brothers, a queen no longer but a chattel which follows the king's treasure. A mere storyteller might have done without Hildeburh, but not the artist who drew the portraits of Wealhtheow and Hygd, not the poet who within the limits of a rapid résumé sought an outlet for his elegiac feeling, not the master of disposition who thus found the means to eliminate a principal character, Hnæf, and to recall without narration the complicated antecedents of the tragedy.

Hildeburh's helpless suffering is a foil to Finn's royal but vain persistence in his attempts to restore the shattered fortunes of his house. He has carried the bitter struggle, which was not of his seeking, to the point where honour was satisfied because Hnæf is fallen in atonement for the death of the Frisian princes. He has learnt to know in Hengest the adversary who has crossed his plans and robbed him of his thanes. He might still make his revenge more complete by adopting the cruel but effective means that are within his power. But he respects the foe who has proved himself invincible in straight fighting, and he seeks to bend this adversary to his will by means that are fair and honourable. It is at this dramatic moment that the poet presents Finn to the audience and it is the moment of his triumph, for Hengest must recognize the necessities of the situation. But the triumph is short-lived—the survivors on both sides are re-united but only to mourn over the ashes of the dead, and the shattered strength of both peoples.

The peace of death reigns through the darkness and silence of winter lurid with the blood-stained memories of the immediate past—and in this setting we see the menacing figure of Hengest, passive as yet but with the passivity of a spent volcano that only awaits the hour to break forth anew. At last spring comes with its call of hope to the hearts of men, and the lust of battle awakens once more in the passionate breast of the man whom Finn had sought to bind with an oath. The symbolic contrast of winter and spring was doubt-less in itself almost enough to enable the poet's hearers to realize the revolution in Hengest's mentality; it hardly needed the rapid parallel with his thoughts of home and revenge, the quick reminder of the sword presented to him, to furnish their minds with an image of the causes that led inevitably to the unforgotten fall of the House of Folcwalda.

I venture to hope that enough has been said to prove that, granted my reconstruction of the Saga and my conception of its relation to the intentions of the epic poet, the Episode (1) presents its matter in a natural and effective grouping; (2) shows the author as an artist of no mean skill in miniature.

APPENDIX I

JUTES OR GIANTS?

A GREAT deal of time, ingenuity and learning has been expended on efforts to prove that the Jutes are mentioned in the Episode—so far as I see without any success, and for a very good reason, namely, because the arguments have been based on a logically insecure foundation.

It requires to be emphasized that the question is raised by the occurrence in the text of the Episode of the word *eotena* three times, and *eotenum* once. Of these *eotena* is ambiguous because it might come either from *eoton*, "giant," or *Éote* (*-as*, *-an*), "Jutes." Unfortunately the situation does not decide the matter one way or the other, since it contains no unambiguous indication which is the preferable meaning of *eotena*. On the other hand *eotenum* is not ambiguous. So long as we remain within the circle of historically given fact it can only be regarded as the dative plural of *eoton*. This testimony, therefore, settles the meaning of *eotena* as being "giants," unless it be proved either that *eotenum* is a scribal error or that it does not refer to the same group of people as *eotena*, or that it is equally ambiguous with *eotena*.

No one, so far as I know, has tried to prove that *eotenum* does not refer to the same people as *eotena*, but attempts have been made to discredit the testimony of the word as follows:

It has been alleged that the scribe may not have understood the tribal name but confused it with the common noun meaning "giants." This is of course quite possible but no one has proved it to be a fact.

It has been alleged that the tribal name may have had a dative plural *Éotenum*. It is of course quite possible that it had such a dative, either of the very rare type represented by *oxnum* or formed on the analogy of *Éotena*. But no one has proved that the form *Éot(e)num* actually existed.

Of course if I bear witness that I enjoyed my dinner to-day a number of statements can be alleged as possibly true, any one of which, if it were really true, would upset my testimony, but unless it can be proved that at least one of these statements actually is true, I can claim that it must be accepted as fact that I did enjoy my dinner. Now it is fact that *eotenum* is the dative plural of *eoton*; it is not fact but only possibility that the scribe confused therewith the tribal name, or that this tribal name had a dative *Éotenum*.

A possibility cannot upset a fact!

Further it has been alleged that the word "giant" applied to either of the contending parties at Finnsburg is inexplicable—but since when has the word inexplicable been tantamount to impossible? I can't explain how the world was created. Must I, therefore, deny that it was created? I can't explain why I prefer beef to mutton. Must I, therefore, doubt that I do prefer beef? Everything has, of course, a reason. Does it follow from that, that nothing is, unless we know the reason? I am ready to assert that to me it is inexplicable that a friend of mine considers it inexplicable that "giant" should be applied in the way above denoted. Have I therewith argued my friend out of existence? *Absit omen.*

Let us, however, examine the logical consequences of rejecting the testimony of *eotenum*. These consequences have, as a matter of fact, been partially drawn by Chambers[1], but only partially, and if we supplement his argument I think the result will be found to be enlightening.

Of course if we neglect the testimony of *eotenum*, it does not follow that thereby *eotena* ceases to be ambiguous. If *eotenum* is allowed to count it solves the ambiguity of *eotena*, but obviously the converse does not hold good, *i.e.* we cannot hold that *eotena* means "Jutes" merely because we deny that *eotenum* forces us to give it the meaning "giants."

We are, therefore, as far as *eotena* is concerned, still faced by ambiguity both of form and situation, *i.e.* we must seek to solve a double pair of ambiguities, viz. "either Jutes or giants" and "either two parties (Frisians plus Danes) of which one has two names, or three parties (Frisians plus Danes plus either Jutes or giants)."

Now in view of the relations between form and content the only hopeful way of trying to solve this double ambiguity is to examine firstly, whether the probability of there having been two parties is greater than that of there having been more than two, or *vice versa*; secondly, what light is thereby thrown on the meaning of *eotena*. It is not very difficult to show, as Chambers has done[2], that on the whole it is more probable that there was a plurality

---

[1] In so far namely as he infers that there were three parties (*Introduction*, p. 268).

[2] *Introduction to Beowulf*, p. 288.

of parties engaged at Finn's burg than that there was only a duality, since in the first place this very commonly occurs in similar situations and in the second place it is indicated by the Fragment through the appearance of Sigeferþ the *Secgena leod*, who as a prince was most likely not alone but accompanied by some of his own people. If we now ask what light this probability throws on the meaning of *eotena*, the answer of course is, next to none, for obviously it is no use knowing that there were several parties unless we can identify one of these as likely to be called by one of the two alternative names, Jutes or giants. Now when we consider the nature of our two sources, it is plain that the only indication of this sort which we have any right to expect would be the presence at Finn's burg of some person who could be shown to have been known as either a Jute or a giant. There is, however, only one indication of this sort. It is afforded by the fact that Hengest bears the same name as the leader of the Jutes who first settled in Kent. If these two personalities could be identified as one and the same person, we should therefore have reason to introduce the Jutes into the Episode with whatever degree of probability attaches to the identification. Now of course the two have been identified with varying degrees of confidence by different writers. This problem it is, however, not necessary for me to discuss, because I cannot personally reject the testimony of *eotenum*. I wish, however, to insist, that even if we do reject that testimony, the only logical ground for connecting the Jutes with the Episode is afforded by the possibility of identifying the two Hengests.

Those critics, however, who reject whatever foundation for argument is afforded by this barely probable identity[1], because it is necessary to their explanation of the Episode that the Jutes should be on the Frisian side—those, I say, who proceed thus have no logical basis for argument about the Jutes at all. They have but the bare hypothesis of the presence of the Jutes and although they can assign a number of reasons why this presence was possible, no number of reasons that only prove something to have been possible can prove it to have been a fact.

Methodically speaking I cannot agree that we have any reason for ruling out the presence of giants in the Finn Episode *a priori*.

---

[1] I cannot consider it as more in spite of the recent contributions by Imelmann (*Forschungen zur altenglischen Poesie*, 1920, pp. 367 ff.) and Nellie Slayton Aurner (*University of Iowa Humanistic Studies*, II, 1921, 56 ff.).

If giants never appeared in Teutonic sagas it would be otherwise, but they are, so to speak, a standing requisite of the supra-natural machinery which is seldom entirely absent. Doubtless to our modern taste it would be more satisfactory to see in the Finn Saga a story of unmixed human interest, and that would be permissible if we could firmly establish the Jutes among its elements. On the other hand, with the circumstances of the Heroic Age no such hard and fast line between human and supernatural is given as is apparent to us. To us it is of course highly regrettable that a fine fellow like Beowulf should have nothing better to do than wrestle with a puerile product of primitive imaginings like Grendel. To us it seems simply inexcusable that the poet should have all that human interest at his command, which was given with the relations of the Danes and the Heatho-Beardan, and actually put it in the background. But he did this and I have no doubt he earned the gratitude of his hearers.

I claim, therefore, that given an indication of the presence of giants in the Episode, even those who hold it to be an ambiguous indication, should examine its possibility before they reject it in favour of something else which is also only possible. We find in the *Nibelungenlied* that the Burgundians have an alternative name which they derive from a super-human race of beings, the Nibelungs. It is true these are dwarfs, but it is not necessary to draw any hard and fast line between dwarfs and giants in the supernatural world of the Teutons. They are manifestations of the same principle, interchangeable with each other and often associated with each other. When Sigfrid wins the Nibelungs' hoard he overcomes twelve giants and a dwarf, Albrich, who has the strength of a giant[1]. In the Scandinavian sources the hoard is derived from a *jǫtunn* (Fafnir)[2] who has a dwarf brother (Regin).

We see, therefore, that a clan of human beings could bear a name that denoted supernatural beings to begin with (giants, dwarfs). I think that is sufficient to establish the possibility that either Frisians or Danes in the Episode might have an alternative name like " giants " (or that a group on either side might have such a name). In other words, it is possible that some story was told about either Finn's or Hnæf's people which connected them with the supernatural world in such a way that they might therefrom derive a designation characteristic of its origin—and " giants " might well be such a designation.

---

[1] *Der Nibelunge Not*, Sievers, 94–99.
[2] *Fáfnismál*, 29 (Neckel).

Given a reconstruction of the Finn Saga such as I have proposed, it is not very difficult to find a place in it for the giants. They can, I believe, be provided for quite as satisfactorily as the Jutes, and, since a hypothesis is a hobby-horse on which I am just as fond of riding as anyone else, I will propound the following for the disbelief of the sceptical. To begin with, as Hogni in the *þiðrikssaga* is fabled to be of elvish descent there can be nothing very surprising in Hengest being an *eotena bearn*. Now if, as is possible, Hnæf derived his treasure from a supra-natural source as Sigfrid did—let us say from the giants—it is further possible that the original owners passed into his vassalage as did Albrich and the dwarfs into that of Sigfrid. In that case giants may have accompanied Hnæf as his body-guard when he went abroad.

An alternative hypothesis would be the following: Hengest was a wandering *wrecca* of uncertain lineage, who had won a great treasure from the giants. He afterwards became a vassal of Hnæf's and placed his riches at this lord's disposal (which is the real situation of Sigfrid at the Burgundian court though it is glossed over in both the Scandinavian and German sources). In this case the hoard would carry the name with it, *i.e.* the owners of the giants' hoard would be called giants, just as the Burgundian owners of the Nibelungs' hoard are called Nibelungs.

In connection with the above I would recall that the dragon's hoard in *Beowulf* is termed *eald enta geweorc* (l. 2774), and that *entisc, eotonisc* are standing epithets for weapons of price.

APPENDIX II

POSTSCRIPT ON LL. 1071–74 A

To solve the problem of the meaning of l. 1072 *a* we have to combine the answers to two questions, viz. "Is it implied that the Eotens were loyal or disloyal?" and "Were the Eotens Frisians or Danes?" The popular solution that the Eotens were Frisians and that they were treacherous makes the answer to the second question depend on the first, by assuming that the sentence contains a litotes and can therefore only point to the treachery of the Eotens, and by arguing further that, if the Eotens were treacherous, they must have been Frisians because the poet would not, owing to his sympathies, have been likely to attribute treachery to the people he called Danes.

In my Essay I followed a line of argument which aimed at showing that the above answer to the first question is not necessary and that of the two possible answers to the second question, one is supported by historical evidence while the other is not. To establish this it was not necessary to examine whether the litotes assumption points to real treachery or not. I was willing for the time being to admit that it did point unequivocally to treachery by someone, since this did not hamper my argument as an advocate of the opposed theory. I permitted myself, therefore, to omit all reference to the important problem of critical method which is raised when we attempt to answer in combination two closely connected questions such as those formulated above. Probably I ought to have resisted that temptation. In any case I will try now to supply the omission.

It will be noticed that the ambiguity underlying the first of the above questions is of a different order from that underlying the second. The one is a formal ambiguity, the other is an ambiguity as to fact. The methodical question, therefore, arises: To which of these should we give the priority in attempting to solve them both?

In my Introduction I recalled the circumstance that in expressing our thoughts we permit ourselves many ambiguities of form; also that in the majority of instances the formal ambiguity raises no difficulty as regards the comprehension of our meaning, for the reason, namely, that behind the formal ambiguity there lies a knowledge of facts which is shared by both speaker and hearer, and which permits no ambiguity of meaning to arise. A condition, therefore, of the effective use of formally ambiguous language is that the concrete facts of the situation in which it is used or to which it refers prevent its meaning being misunderstood. Now this being so it is surely obvious that the reason why we must be doubtful about the formal implications of the sentence in *Beowulf* is that we do not know who the Eotens are. To solve the formal ambiguity we must therefore seek to remove the obstacle to its solution, *i.e.* we must frame a hypothesis of the facts from which we can deduce the form of the sentence, and explain its ambiguity, not *vice versa*. We must make the answer to the first of the above questions depend on the answer to the second. Further, since the word *treowe* is ambiguous, as noted above, and since it is possible for a person to be loyal to one side while he is disloyal to their opponents, we must allow for the possibility that the facts were such that, even were they known, the formal ambiguity of the sentence might still remain, *i.e.* we must make allowance for a situation with which ambiguity of fact as well as ambiguity of form is given, in which the Eotens might appear to be both loyal and disloyal.

Under these conditions it appears to me a suspicious circumstance that the popular theory derives the facts from the form and I must enquire whether the road from this starting-point to the conclusion is as undeviating as seems generally to be assumed.

If we take the sentence of the text both as litotes and a merely abstract indication of the nature of the relations between Hildeburh and the Eotens, then the inference that treachery was involved is practically unavoidable. This is the natural thing for the modern reader to do because he knows nothing about the concrete events referred to. But the poet had something more than a knowledge that in the abstract the situation in which Hildeburh and the Eotens were involved was disagreeable to them in a specific way. He had a picture in his mind of a concrete situation and concrete events, and the statement he makes about Hildeburh and the Eotens is not merely abstract, it is a summing up of the situation in which he saw them and the events which occurred therein. A clear idea then of the possibilities of what he meant can only be gained by envisaging the nature of the concrete possibilities which might thus be summed up.

Now there can be little doubt that a presupposition of the Episode is a situation in which by a concrete act the *sibb ond treow* between Frisians and Danes was broken. The question therefore arises: Of what nature may a concrete act be, which amounts to a breach of the peace sufficient to entail tragical consequences? The answer of course is, it may very well be a deliberate act of treachery but it may also be an accidental act, an "unfortunate incident," a happening which could not be foreseen or provided for.

When some years ago the Russian nation sent out an expedition which was to result in the destruction of their fleet by the Japanese, I do not remember any anticipation that the first act of that fleet would be to open fire on British fishermen. This, however, did occur and it was one of those "unfortunate incidents" which often enough have led to war between nations. It was certainly a breach of *treow* but it was just as certainly not deliberate treachery.

So long as we have no testimony to the contrary, it is quite possible that the *treow* between Frisians and Danes was broken in some such accidental manner as I have represented in my reconstruction of the Saga. That is to say it is possible that it was broken in the first place by an individual acting in unforeseen circumstances as such, and without any "mandate" from the clan to which he belonged. For such breaches the community to which the individual belongs must often assume, through its representatives, a technical responsibility, *i.e.* must admit that it as a whole has broken the peace and shape its conduct accordingly. I claim that my reconstruction shows the possibility of Hildeburh having taken the view of the Eotens' conduct that "faith unfaithful kept them falsely true." If the circumstances the poet had in mind were at all such as I have depicted, it would indeed be difficult for Hildeburh to distinguish between the guilt of the individual whose outburst of resentment at an unpremeditated insult laid the train for the following tragedy, and the guilt of his companions who backed him up to the end. Their undoubted loyalty among themselves might then very well appear to her as disloyalty to the other side, who were naturally their friends, and the poet sympathizing with her standpoint as a mother and sister, and as a woman outside the fierce unreasoning quarrel of the men, might possibly, accenting the proper name, have said, "Hildeburh indeed had grounds to condemn the Eotens for disloyalty." He could easily have said this, too, without feeling that it would convey a reflection on the side with which he sympathized, for, if the tragedy sprang from accident and both sides, therefore, were equally free of guilt, he could not have any qualms about alluding to those he favoured as the cause of offence if everybody knew that they were the innocent cause.

On the basis of the above argumentation I believe that the litotes explanation of l. 1071 does not necessarily compel us to regard treachery as the origin of the quarrel between the Danes and Frisians. Furthermore, although for the reasons assigned in my Essay I consider it the less likely of two alternative explanations, I hold that it can be harmonized with the reconstruction of the Saga which I have already made. In other words, I regard it as an advantage of my reconstruction that because it provides for the ambiguity of fact referred to above (p. 145), it permits us to deduce the text of ll. 1071–72 *a*, whether we take the passage in question one way or the other, *i.e.* whether we take the negation it contains as "serious" or "ironical," as merely privative or a litotes. But this is not all. If the litotes hypothesis does not lead necessarily to the conception of treachery on the one side or the other, neither does it lead of necessity to the popular translation of *unsynnum* in l. 1072 *b* as "guiltless," *i.e.* to the conception that this word refers to the subject of the sentence, as if it were an adjective, not an adverb. I have argued that *unsynnum* means "without feud" for reasons assigned above. But even if these reasons are not sufficient, even if it be judged impossible to start here from the sense of "feud" for *syn* and therefore necessary to start from the commoner sense of "guilt," my refusal to see in this word an uncalled-for reference to Hildeburh's innocence is still justifiable. For *unsynnum* is undeniably an adverb, and belongs therefore syntactically to the verb, not the subject. Taking "guilt" as the ground meaning, what the sentence therefore says is, "guiltlessly she was deprived...," *i.e.* the manner of the action denoted is asserted to have been "guiltless." All the sentence therefore conveys explicitly through its form amounts to this, "The actions by which she was deprived of her dear ones were guiltless." I admit, of course, the possibility that this form of sentence might be used to imply that the actions were guiltless as far as the participation of the subject alone was concerned— but it is only a possibility, and as such has to be weighed against the other possibility that it may refer not to the subject, who, since the verb is in the passive, is really the object, but to the actual doers of the actions. It appears, therefore, that if *unsynnum* can be explained as "without feud between the parties concerned," it might also be explained as "without guilt on either side," and this latter would also be in harmony with the hypothesis I have adopted throughout, that the ghastly nature of the tragedy in the Finn Saga was enhanced by the fact that it all sprang from an accident.

APPENDIX III

THE EMPLOYMENT OF *.AC.* IN *BEOWULF*

ONE of the most active forms of the association of ideas is that between such as are antithetic to one another, *i.e.* between ideas which exclude each other, in the sense that they cannot be truly affirmed together of the same thing at the same time. The most obvious type of such associations is that between extremes or opposites, *e.g. good* and *bad, wet* and *dry, long* and *short.* They can, however, also exist between extremes and means, *e.g. ugly* or *beautiful* and *plain.* Furthermore, they can occur between the individual aspects of things in so far as these may be thought of in opposition to each other. Thus a thing cannot be conceived as both the one and the other thing at one and the same time. In this sense a part may not only be mutually exclusive of another part but also of the whole to which it belongs. For this reason "all are not coming" usually implies "but some are," namely, because "all are coming" and "some are coming" are in the sense indicated mutually exclusive. "Some are not coming" should imply for the same reason a choice between "all are coming" and "the rest are coming," but is generally accepted in the latter sense. On this relation depends the analysis of "both" into "not only the one but (also) the other" (instead of "one *and* the other"), due to the fact that "the one" is excluded by "both" and also by "the other"; so that we have "not only I but you also," to bear witness to opposition between "I" and "you" (or "both of us"). Similarly John and James, the French and the English, and so on, may be antithetic pairs.

When an association of this kind enters into a judgment of fact, the whole can only be expressed by means of two co-ordinate propositions. These may be stated, according as the judgment is tentative or decisive, in two forms of compound utterance, which may be illustrated schematically as follows:

(1) (Either) *A* is *B*, or it is *C*.
(2) *A* is not *B*, (but) it is *C*.

The two types are distinguished by the contrast that in (1) both propositions are affirmative, while in (2) one must necessarily be negative.

In the following we are concerned with the latter of these types, regarded as a grammatical phenomenon, to which I propose to give the name "antithetic expansion." It is represented concretely by examples like "He isn't crying, he's laughing," "Don't dawdle but be quick," "I needn't but you must." ("Expansion" has, of course, just been used in the sense in which we can speak of a compound sentence as the expansion of a simple sentence.)

From the above type of statement we must distinguish another, which formally speaking often greatly resembles it, and to which I give the name "concessive expansion." It differs from the preceding by the fact that we have here ideas expressed which are conceived as *usually* excluding each other though they do not *necessarily* do so. Examples are: "She is not pretty but charming." "He is not strong but he fights well." There is, however, this great difference between the two that an "antithetic expansion" always involves a *true* negative[1], *i.e.* a proposition which is equivalent to the logical formula "*A* is-not *B*"; while in the "concessive expansion" both sentences are really affirmative, although it is permissible for either to have any linguistic form which can be taken to mean "*A* is not-*B*." Hence it is a matter of indifference whether I say "He is not strong..." or "He is weak (but he fights well)." Both sentences may in fact be "grammatical" negatives, *e.g.* "He is unwell but not depressed."

Note. The above remarks are of course to be understood in the light of the considerations on negation which I have formulated in my Essay. See above, pp. 26 ff.

On account of the relation between the underlying associated ideas the expression of an antithetic expansion is logically equivalent to an act of choice by which one alternative is rejected in favour of another. Hence we find that the negated proposition is equivalent to the minor premiss, and the affirmative proposition to the conclusion, of a syllogism whose major premiss is "Either *X* or *Y* (where *X* and *Y* denote propositions which cannot be true together)." Thus: "I'm not crying, I'm laughing," corresponds to the syllogism "either I am laughing or crying, but I am not crying, therefore I am laughing." The underlying association of an antithetic expansion has therefore a logical content which is expressible by the formula "Either *X* or *Y*"; or, since *X* and *Y* are based on contraries, more comprehensively by "Either *A* is *B* or *C*," or "Either *B* or *C* is *A*," according as the contrary

---

[1] This is so even when the first sentence is a "grammatical" negative, *i.e.* formally an affirmative. In Modern English the grammatical often takes the place of the real negative, thus "none of them did" may be said instead of "they didn't," or "they had no cause" instead of "they hadn't (any) cause."

ideas are subject or predicate. When the underlying contraries are aspects of individuality the second form of the formula is usually applicable, *e.g.* "I needn't do it, but you must." This gives us a useful and convenient means of testing whether a given statement is a disjunctive expansion or not. If we can show that it involves alternative propositions which exclude each other, then this question is answered affirmatively.

Note. I do not attempt to solve the difficult question whether the speaker actually feels the logical implications of disjunctive expansion. Possibly the great regularity with which the syllogistic order, first negative, then affirmative, is adhered to, is evidence that he has a slight sensation of making a choice.

In *Beowulf .ac.* stands regularly between a preceding negative and an immediately following affirmative sentence. The few exceptions to this rule are of such a nature that their discussion need not be dissociated from the instances which come under the rule. The first thing which I have now to show is that *.ac.* in *Beowulf* is always an external sign of the phenomenon I have called "antithetic expansion." When this is proved it will be time to consider what light it throws on the function of the word.

There are two main obstacles which obscure the recognition of "antithetic expansion" in *Beowulf.* Firstly, this form of statement is used for narrative and descriptive purposes to an extent and in ways which from a modern standpoint are unusual, and therefore may lead us to expect something else more in accordance with modern habits of expression. Secondly, while such expansion is always based on propositions of a logically simple content, the expression of these may for various reasons become so complicated as almost to hide that content from view. Of course both obstacles may present themselves at one and the same time, but the examples can be discussed under the separate headings indicated without loss of clearness.

It will not be necessary to deal in detail with all the instances. Viewed from a modern standpoint these come under certain types which appear to be different from one another. It will be sufficient to consider these varying types and show that they all conform to the characteristics of "antithetic expansion." In this way I shall take up under I the employment of disjunctive expansion in ways that are unexpected to a modern reader, under II the complications which disguise the underlying simple propositions.

I

I deal first with the common type of instances exemplified at l. 740 (The monster had no thought of delay but quickly seized a sleeping warrior) of which it has been asserted that the same thought is expressed twice, once positively, once negatively[1]. It is hardly necessary to burden the poet with such triviality. Obviously the negative sentence in such instances only expresses the same thought as the affirmative if we assume that its function is to imply the affirmative "*A* is not-*B*." Why, however, make that assumption? If we take it literally it is a denial that *A* is *B* and that is a different thought from the affirmative *A* is *C*. The example above quoted can be reduced to the alternatives: Either he hesitated or acted quickly (and so in similar instances), *i.e.* the poet had in mind the very real distinction between hesitant and decisive action.

The cases in which *.ac.* seems to have a confirmatory function ("begründendes" *.ac.*[2]) are also, I hold, to be regarded as belonging to the category of those in which the modern reader fails to perceive antithetic expansion on account of the strength of his feeling for the implications of the negative sentence. It often happens that the affirmative which we feel to be implied by the negative sentence in *Beowulf* is a consequence, of which the following affirmative introduced by *.ac.* may be regarded as the antecedent. When this is so, "*A* is not *B* but *C*" is for our feeling often equivalent to "*A* is *D* because *A* is *C*." Thus *Beowulf*, l. 109, *Ne gefeah he þære fæhðe, ac he hine feor forwræc, Metod*, may convey, "He was unhappy (*i.e.* he was miserable) because the Lord punished him." It is quite plain, however, that to the author the two propositions *He gefeah þære fæhðe* and *Metod hine forwræc* must have been mutually exclusive, and we can, I think, on that account assume with certainty that the assertion of the one necessarily entailed the denial of the other. It is not difficult to see that the example just quoted is reducible to "Not (he was happy) but (he was punished),"[3] *i.e.* to the formula "Not (*A* is *B*) but (*A* is *C*)," and it will be found that all similar examples are reducible in the same way. In such cases it is only when we take "*A* is-not *B*" as implying "*A* is not-*B*" that the causal relation forces itself into our minds and the two propositions strike us as harmonious instead of contrasted. If, however, we resist this

---

[1] Schücking, *Satzverknüpfung in Beowulf*, p. 92.
[2] Cp. Schücking, *loc. cit.*
[3] Cp. below, p. 153 f.

tendency, I think it will be found that the .ac. formula does not here correspond to the style of expression which we have in English when a negative sentence is followed by an affirmative introduced by "because" or "for," but to another quite different style, that namely in which a negative sentence is followed by an affirmative introduced by "on the contrary." Let us test this by translating a few passages:

l. 863. Indeed they did not disparage their own lord; on the contrary, that was a good king!

l. 2505. By no means did he succeed in bringing the booty to the Frisian king; on the contrary, he fell in the fray.

l. 2828. The coiled dragon might no longer control the hoarded treasure; on the contrary, blades of steel had carried him off.

l. 109. He had no pleasure in consequence of that feud; on the contrary, God drove him away from the abodes of men.

l. 446. If I am killed, thou wilt not have to hide my head (? bury me); on the contrary, he will take me, his blood-stained booty.

l. 804. No war-bill would touch the wretch; on the contrary, he had put a spell on the weapons of victory.

I find confirmation of the above in the following. The instances of the so-called "begründendes .ac." are not the only ones which can suggest the existence of a causal relation between the negative and the affirmative sentence. There are a number of instances in which the content of the negative sentence, if we do not resist the tendency to take the latter as implying the affirmative "*A* is not-*B*," then appears as the antecedent of which the following affirmative is the consequence. The result is that .ac. apparently means "consequently," and as a matter of fact the German translator Gering in at least two such cases renders it by "drum,"[1] while in one instance he has a "so." I mention as clear illustrations of this phenomenon the following, in all of which it will be found that if .ac. be translated by "accordingly" it gives good sense: ll. 601, 683, 1085, 2525, 2675, 2697, 2850. This list might be added to; as it stands, it is sufficient to prove that, *if* we have reason to assume that .ac. meant "because," there is likewise reason to believe that it meant "consequently." Both these things can hardly be true together. It follows that when the poet used an *ac*, he can hardly have done so because a causal relation was present in his mind.

On the other hand, we should bear in mind that a speaker may have either of the following motives for negating the proposition

[1] Cp. also Schuchardt, *Die Negation in Beowulf*, Berlin, 1910, p. 73.

"*A* is *B*." He may either perceive that "*A* is *B*" is excluded by the contrary proposition "*A* is *C*," or he may perceive that "*A* is not-*B*" (or "*A* is not"). It follows, therefore, that when "*A* is not-*B*" is a cause or consequence of "*A* is *C*," the speaker will have a choice between saying either "*A* is-not *B* because, or consequently, *A* is *C*" or "*A* is-not *B* but *C*." Whether he chooses the one or the other will depend upon whether it is uppermost in his mind that "*A* is *C*" excludes "*A* is *B*," or that "*A* is *C*" stands in a causal relation to "*A* is not-*B*." Hence in Modern English we can say either "He is not happy because he has been severely punished," or "He is not happy; on the contrary he has been severely punished," and it will be noted that in the first instance we have before our consciousness the *agreement* between "not happy" and "punished," and in the second, the *opposition* between "happy" and "punished."

This seems to me to solve Schücking's doubt expressed in the following: "Eine andere Frage aber ist, ob psychologisch d.h. im Bewusstsein des Sprechenden hier die Anschauung einer Kausalität vorlag, und von andern Fällen des aufhebenden *ac* im Bewusstsein differenziert wurde."[1]

II

I have now to deal with the causes which obscure the exact nature of the propositions underlying an antithetic expansion in *Beowulf*. Such obscurity may arise in two ways. It may, namely, result when a proposition is not explicitly stated but conveyed by implication; or it may result when the proposition is amplified into something more than the bare expression of its logical content. Of course both causes of complication may be effective at the same time, but it will suffice to consider their respective characteristics separately.

Latent Implications

In the test formula "Either *A* is *B* or *C*," both propositions have the same subject. Some difficulty arises in applying it because the corresponding expressions in *Beowulf* by no means have necessarily the same subject, *i.e.* the logical subject is not necessarily the grammatical subject. Owing to this change of subject the modern reader easily gets the suggestion of a double antithesis, namely between the predicates *and* between the subjects. In consequence, such expansions seem to be reducible to a formula "Either *A* or *B* is either *C* or *D*" with the solution expressed in

[1] *Loc. cit.* p. 91.

the form: "*A* is not *C* but *B* is *D*." Since, however, "*A* is *C*" is not here necessarily excluded by "*B* is *D*," but only on the condition that "*A* is not-*C*" is causally related to "*B* is *D*," the further effect on the modern reader is that he is apt in such cases to take the *.ac.* as indication of this causal relation where present, thus leading to a view which above I have tried, I hope successfully, to dispose of. When one notes, however, that in such cases the subject of one sentence generally appears in the other in the guise of an accusative or dative or the like, it becomes easy to reduce them by the above test. Thus (l. 109), "He had no joy of the consequences but God drove him away" transforms into "he was driven away by God"; and l. 1300, "Beowulf wasn't there, but another resting place had been allotted him" becomes "he had been allotted another resting place." The same applies to an example like l. 2697, *Ne hedde he þæs heafolan, ac sio hand gebarn modiges mannes*, with a genitive as expression for the logical subject. It reduces, namely, to "Either he heeded for his head (*i.e.* his safety) or he got his hand burned." That is to say the boldness with which Wiglaf attacked is asserted by indicating its outward sign (cp. remarks below), the wound to his hand. Obviously this explanation applies equally if we take "heafolan" to refer to the dragon[1].

With this distinction between logical and grammatical subject in mind we can easily resolve the somewhat startling example at l. 1576, *næs seo ecg fracod hilde-rince, ac he hraþe wolde Grendle forgyldan guð-ræsa fela*. The dative in the negative sentence expresses the logical subject. We therefore get, "The hero did not contemn the sword (*i.e.* did not hesitate to use it) but quickly set about paying Grendel back."

This last instance is a good example for the unity of motive and deed, cp. next paragraph.

There can be little doubt that, where antecedent and consequent are continuously manifested and are obviously present as a matter of everyday experience, they form a whole which the naïve observer does not resolve into parts connected by the logical relation of causality, *i.e.* in this case he is conscious that the parts belong together, but he does not think of the abstract relation between them. It is due to this that in the expression of thought either antecedent or consequent can stand for the whole to which both belong. This is a common feature in the expression of dis-

---

[1] Cp. the note in Chambers' edition. I remark that it is not necessary, as done here, to denote the *.ac.* clause as parenthetic. Since it expresses boldness the following *þæt* clause in l. 2699 joins on directly.

junctive expansions in *Beowulf*. Thus the motive and the act are a whole, hence (l. 740) instead of "He did not delay" we get "He didn't think of delaying" (cp. Modern English, "I had no intention of doing it"). Similarly in the example at l. 2308. Again, a bad king is an unpopular king, his badness and the attitude of his subjects to him are parts of a whole. Hence instead of "He was not a bad but a good king," we get (l. 863), "They did not disparage him but that was a good king."

The symbolic style of expression to which this phenomenon gives rise does not necessarily trouble the modern reader. The naïve standpoint which it reflects is not quite foreign to us even yet. But occasionally it gives rise to difficulties; and it will be well to illustrate their solution by a couple of examples:

l. 2223. *Nealles mid gewealdum wyrm-hord abræc sylfes willum . . . ac for þrea-nedlan . . . hete-swengeas fleah.*

The alternatives are "he acted either voluntarily or of necessity"; his action, however, breaks up into two parts, viz. theft and flight, of which one is the consequence of the other. The consequential part stands for the whole in the negative sentence, the causal part has the same function in the positive.

l. 1509. *Swa he ne mihte (no he þæs modig wæs) wæpna gewealdan, ac hine wundra þæs fela swencte on sunde.*

Owing to the fact that Beowulf is swimming downwards through the water, he cannot at the same time use his weapons and must depend on his armour to protect him from the attacks of the mere-wolf and the other monsters. The alternatives are therefore "Beowulf's defence was either active or passive." An active defence involves ability to use one's weapons, consequently this ability is denied in the negative sentence. A passive defence involves here being thrashed by one's enemies and this is asserted in the affirmative. If in l. 1509 we read, as above, *þæs* for the *þæm* of the MS. and following Schücking, take *no* with *wæs*, we get the meaning "he was not excited on that account," *i.e.* Beowulf had foreseen his inability to resist the monsters while engaged in swimming, and was not worried by it[1].

l. 683. *Nat he þara goda þæt he me ongean slae . . . ac wit on niht sculon secge ofersittan.*

The alternatives are "Either both of us will use or avoid the use of weapons." Understanding the use of weapons and using them go together in the poet's thought. Hence, when he denies that "one understands their use" he is free to assert that "both will

[1] Cf. below, p. 156.

do without," since "He will not" is also part of a whole here, namely, "He and I will not"; this being due to the fact that the speaker is already bound by his *ʒielp* not to use weapons, cp. ll. 435 ff., 679.

Overt Implications

(*a*) The negative statement is implied by an affirmative: l. 2899 (*lyt*, by litotes = *nealles*); l. 438 *b* (*ic þæt forhicge = ic nylle*); l. 1448—this last is a complicated case and calls for discussion. The poet is here plainly concerned to motivate why Beowulf, in contrast with what had been told about him when engaged in the swimming match with Breca, makes no active resistance to the sea-monsters while diving downwards to the bottom of the mere. As comes out later, Beowulf's first aim is to reach the mere-wolf's submarine fastness, and, while forcing a way thither, he will trust to his armour to protect him from the attacks of the enemy[1]. Corslet and helmet are consequently personified as trusty allies of the swimmer and to each the poet assigns a double function, namely, its usual one and a new one given by the circumstances. The gist of the passage from ll. 1443 to 1454 is then "The corslet was to do the swimming and guard the hero's trunk, but the helmet was to lead the way (*mere-grundas mengan* in antithesis to *sund cunnian*) and protect his head." We have thus a double antithesis of the "one and the other of two" order[2], firstly, between the parts of a whole (armour), secondly, between their several functions. Now it is obvious that in these circumstances the affirmation of one part's function implies two negations, *e.g.* "the corslet guards the trunk" implies "the corslet does not guard the head" as well as "the helmet does not guard the trunk," further that these negations are likewise implied by "the helmet guards the head." The two affirmative statements may therefore be conceived as united by their mutual relation to either of the statements which both exclude. That is to say, in such circumstances a statement like "The corslet guards the body" can immediately suggest "It does not guard the head," and this in thought (although it need not be spoken) can supply the transition to "the helmet guards the head," by way of a "but" instead of an "and." To put it otherwise, a co-ordinate parataxis like "The corslet guards the trunk, the helmet guards the head" (*i.e.* one whose content is unified by a double antithesis) can be synthetized either by mere summation of the two parts (*e.g.* by "and") or

---

[1] Cp. my remarks on l. 1509, p. 155.   [2] Cp. above, p. 148.

by a word expressing the mutual relation of both to other statements whose negative quality is implicit in the antithetic content to which all belong. Such a word in Modern English is "but," in the Anglo-Saxon of *Beowulf* it is *.ac.*

There is still a circumstance which is of interest as bearing out the above. Denoting the antithetic parts of the whole by A and A', their double antithetic (new and old) functions by B, B' and C, C', the logical arrangement of the contents of ll. 1443–54 would be, "A is $B + C$ but A' is $B' + C'$." There is a *formal* correspondence to this, in that the compound propositions before and after the *.ac.* are expressed symmetrically by a main sentence followed by a relative clause. But the contents are reversed, so that we get "A is B, which is C but A' is C', which is B'." The poet began naturally enough with A's (the corslet's) new function, to which he added its old function, as a permanent attribute, in a relative sentence. The old function of A then evidently suggested *its* antithesis, the old function of A', so that, since he held to the formal parallelism, he expressed this in a main sentence and added the new function of A' in a relative sentence. This change of order, due to attraction of one idea by another which, in the context, plainly excludes it, shows that the underlying antithetic relations of the content were really active in the poet's mind.

(*b*) The negative sentence is suppressed, but is implicit in the situation. There is but one example which occurs at l. 1990 in dialogue between Hygelac and Beowulf. *Ac þu Hroðgare widcuðne wean wihte gebettest* is undoubtedly a question on account of the *wihte*. Due to its ordinary use in negative sentences the meaning of *wihte* must have been indefinite, *i.e.* "to a degree," or "to any degree, at all." This would prevent it from being used in affirmative sentences but allow its use in questions; cp. "I didn't at all," "Did you at all?" but "I did to some extent." Hygelac therefore asks: "But did you at all improve Hrothgar's wretched condition?"

Hygelac has already asked "How did you get on at Heorot?" This implies, "Did you succeed or fail?" Now Hygelac, in Beowulf's return, has evidence that Beowulf did not fail altogether but he can hardly believe in a complete success. His anticipation of the reply that he expects might occur to himself as "You did not fail but you succeeded to some extent." It would, however, hardly be polite to hint at the alternative of failure, and therefore the negation is suppressed. Since, however, the affirmation is only a suggestion of his own that still requires confirmation, it comes out as a question, followed by the grounds for the speaker's hesitation. The same sort of hesitancy, due to the unexpected, comes out in the analogous modern greeting, "So you're here, are you?"

Amplification

Under "amplification" I understand the supplying of circumstantial details over and beyond what is necessary to express fully the logical content of either of the contrasted propositions in a disjunctive expansion. Here an interesting syntactical phenomenon frequently comes to view. It often occurs namely that an additional detail—which is of course logically of minor importance—is not subordinated to the main proposition. This can take place in two ways. Either the addition is stated in a main sentence to which the real proposition is added in a dependent sentence, or the addition is treated as a major predicate to which the logical predicate is subordinated as if it were only an accompanying circumstance. Of the latter we have an example in the passage at l. 2181. Here it is evident that logically speaking the affirmative proposition is, "But he was by the grace of God the strongest of men,"[1] which by reversing the relation of the major and minor predicates becomes, "but he held the immense gift that God gave him by the greatest strength." Another example occurs at l. 135, *Næs hit lengra fyrst, ac ymb ane niht eft gefremede morð-beala mare.* The alternatives are "Either it was a long or short time till...." "It was a short time till he did it" becomes "He did it in a short time (defined as one night later)." The curious comparative in the negated statement might be due to another aspect of the extremes mixing itself in the poet's thought with the already mentioned alternatives, viz. "Either it was a longer or shorter time than expected."

More frequently we meet with the first mode of amplification (subordination of the real proposition to a main sentence). In such cases the real proposition is introduced as a particular instance of a more general phenomenon, *e.g.* as something well known (l. 2923 *b, ac wæs wide cuð þætte...*); as something marvellous (ll. 771–775, the negated proposition is introduced by *þa wæs wundor micel þæt*); as a matter of personal experience (ll. 809 ff., negative introduced by *þa þæt onfunde þæt*; similarly, ll. 1522 *b*–25); as an instance of God's grace (l. 1661, affirmative introduced by *ac me geuðe ylda waldend þæt*), and so on. No doubt it

---

[1] Since strength and gentleness proverbially go together, this symbolizes the gentleness which is opposed to the *hreoh sefa* of the preceding line. The alternatives are "Either he was savage or gentle."

is this more general nature of the additional circumstance which explains its syntactical superordination over the logical main proposition. The modern style prefers to keep such things in their logical place as far as possible; thus ll. 771 ff. is better translated "For a wonder (*not*: it was a wonder that) the dwelling did not fall, but...." When the general formula precedes the negative, the question arises whether *both* propositions are syntactically dependent on it. This question can hardly be decided with certainty[1], but it seems to me probable that in such cases the affirmative proposition was not felt as syntactically subordinated. In the passage just quoted, for instance, it can hardly be implied that it was a marvel that the hall was firmly built. It might have been a marvel of course that it was "so" firmly built, but this sense can hardly be assigned to *þæs fæste*, the alternatives being "Either it fell or was *too* firmly built to fall."

(*a*) (Amplification of the negative sentence.) Rather complicated is the instance at ll. 2518 *b*–23 *a*: *Nolde ic sweord beran, wæpen to wyrme, gif ic wiste hu wið ðam aglæcean elles meahte gylpe wiðgripan, swa ic gio wið Grendle dyde, ac ic þær heaðu-fyres hates wene, oreðes ond attres.*

This, however, resolves itself simply enough if we remember, firstly, that Beowulf in the adventure with the dragon departs from his own precedent in his adventure with Grendel. The poet obviously regrets that Beowulf cannot conquer a fire-spitting drake by mere strength of arm, and feels that his action here is rather out of character. Consequently he makes him apologize to his followers for bearing to the fray the shield which he had had specially constructed (ll. 2337–39) for the purpose. (This may, indeed, be somewhat naïve, but it shows at any rate that the author was careful to assign motives which would not damage the unity of his hero's character.) Secondly, we must bear in mind that compulsion eliminates desire: "I must" excludes "I would," whence the common formula in Modern English, "I would not do this, if I could help it, but I must."

The poet preserves the unity of character by giving Beowulf the desire to fight on this occasion as he had formerly done, plus common sense enough to perceive that it is out of the question that he should do so. He throws his hero's apology into a form which is exactly parallel to the modern formula I have just quoted, allowing for the fact that the compulsion is symbolized by its cause ("I must," > "I expect hot flames") and that "if I could help it"

---

[1] Cp. Schücking, *loc. cit.* p. 93 (Anm. 4).

is swelled into "If I knew how I might otherwise accomplish my boast against the monster as I formerly did against Grendel."

(*b*) Interesting amplifications of the affirmative proposition occur at ll. 1661 and 3011.

In l. 1661 the contrasted propositions are simply "I accomplished the deed with Hrunting" and "I did it with another sword." The former is excluded by "I couldn't do anything with Hrunting." As regards the latter: "I did the deed with another sword" naturally calls for an explanation of what sword is meant, but "which by the grace of God I saw hanging on the wall" is made into the main sentence[1], thus leading to, "but God granted me that I saw an old sword," on to which is tacked "(and) that I swung it," the sense being completed by a further asyndetic clause (there should be no full stop after *gebrægd* of course), "slew there in the fight, as opportunity offered, the owners of the house."

In the case of l. 3011 the speaker chooses between the alternatives "Either the whole or a part is to be burned." The affirmative is amplified into a dramatic pointing at the treasure with an enumeration of its salient parts, ending: "these shall the flames devour."

(*c*) Amplification in both propositions:

Line 708 offers a very difficult example, which, however, may be solved, I think, as follows. The alternative propositions, "They were saved" and "They were destroyed," are parts of wholes in the poet's thought which may be represented thus: "They were saved because Beowulf was watching" and "They perished when God wished." In the affirmative sentence the antecedent is put for the whole and elaborated into "he, watchful and determined, was awaiting the outcome," which is plain enough in view of the fact, that the outcome has already been announced[2]. The negative becomes "the enemy hadn't any chance to kill them when God did not wish it," and since this has obviously a general as well as a particular application it is introduced by the generalizing formula "that was known to men." I may say that it seems to me absurd to see in the negative sentence here a concessive statement[3], thus turning it into something like "Although by common knowledge they were in God's keeping, yet Beowulf stayed awake." The common sense of "Trust in God and keep your powder dry" would appeal to the *Beowulf* poet.

In the passage at l. 595 the alternatives are "Either you are

---

[1] Cp. above, p. 158.　　　　　　　　　[2] Cp. l. 696 f.

[3] Clark Hall, *Beowulf* (1911), p. 43.

brave or a coward." "You are not brave" is conveyed by the common recriminatory formula "If you were *B*, then this would not have happened (*i.e.* you are not *B*)," the if-clause being magnified into "if your spirit were as determined as you count it yourself." After this the affirmative is implied by its consequential negative, "Your opponent does not need to be afraid of (you or) your people, *i.e. you* are afraid of him." Both propositions are introduced by "generalizing" formulae[1]. It is, of course, unnecessary to begin a new sentence with *.ac.*

(*d*) A peculiar type of amplification is apparent in the passage ll. 691–702 *a*. The editors usually break the period by a full stop in the middle of l. 696, but this is unnecessary. We have, I believe, to recognize that here one proposition is contrasted with two others, both of which exclude it[2]. It is pretty plain that in the first place the poet wishes to emphasize that the coming victory over Grendel was gained not by the efforts of *all* the Geats but by the strength of *one*. The main antithesis therefore gives the alternatives "Either *all* contributed to the victory or *one* gained it for all," of which the first has to be eliminated. The affirmative, by reversing the logical relation of subordination, becomes "all triumphed over their enemy by one man's strength" introduced by the usual pious reference to God's grace. Since the whole is an anticipation of events yet to be related, the alternative is eliminated by a reference to the present state of mind of Beowulf's companions. This suggests the minor alternatives, "Either all expected to survive or they had authority to the contrary." Thus we get "none of them expected (with the usual substitution of the grammatical negative for 'all did not expect') ever to return home; on the contrary, they had heard of the direful destruction of the Danes." The statement "all contributed to the victory" is therefore eliminated by denying to *all* of them[3] the necessary motive of success, *i.e.* self-confidence, the hope of surviving.

When in Modern English a proposition is to be excluded in favour of a major and a minor contrary, the latter can be intercalated by means of "on the contrary," which leaves the reference of a succeeding "but" to the introductory negation clear. In this way we get a smooth translation of the whole of this complicated

---

[1] Cp. above, p. 158.

[2] Schuchardt has already suggested (*Negation im Beowulf*, p. 75), that the second *.ac.*, like the first, stands "in Anlehnung an die negative Aussage."

[3] That is to say, not inclusively but exclusively of Beowulf, the one member who is thought of in antithesis to the whole group.

passage, as follows: "Not one of them supposed that he would ever revisit his dear home...on the contrary[1], they had heard that formerly murderous death had carried off all too many of the Danish people in that wine-hall; but God granted them the woven fabric of success in battle, to the people of the Weder-Geats solace and help, so that they all triumphed over their enemy (*feond* is of course singular) through the strength of one man and his might alone."

From a modern standpoint the major expansion seems to be a concessive one (= Although they despaired of success, yet they conquered). That the poet did not feel it so, is proved by the fact that the negative sentence also belongs to the minor expansion, which cannot possibly be taken as concessive. This negative, consequently, is a striking illustration of my remarks above (p. 155) on the unity of motive and deed—the lack of the proper motive eliminates the corresponding action.

A final remark must be devoted to adversative *.ac.*, so called. For this function Schücking[2] quotes six examples. As regards three of these (ll. 595, 2522, 696 *b*) I have just shown above that they can be explained satisfactorily in the ordinary manner. A fourth, l. 1085 *b*, has been treated in the Essay. The two that remain are ll. 601 *b* and 2973, and both of these can also be shown to be not different from the rest.

As regards l. 601 *b*, *ac ic him Geata sceal eafoð ond ellen ungeara nu guðe gebeodan* is not to be separated from the immediately preceding: *secce ne weneþ to Gar-Denum.* The choice of propositions is "Either he will be opposed by the Danes or the Geats." The first is denied by implication in "He (Grendel) has no expectation of fight from the Danes" (Beowulf is obviously skating on thin ice here and must not let his contempt for Unferþ lead him into being too severe on the Danes); the affirmative is put quite plainly, Beowulf taking the responsibility for the Geats' behaviour on his own shoulders—"but I shall soon show him the valour of the Geats." It is worth noting by the way how in this passage, from ll. 590–603 *a*, the poet very neatly compiles a long period of thirteen and a half lines with the help of three *ac*'s (in ll. 595, 599, 601). His editors, however, seem rather unwilling to give him credit for this feat, there not being a single recent one (so far as I have observed) who allows him to get to the end without interpolating a full stop somewhere. The passage at ll. 691–

---

[1] Clark Hall here translates *.ac.* by "nay," which is also good.
[2] *Loc. cit.* p. 92.

702 *a* should be compared[1]. The passage at l. 2973 is plain enough! "Either Wulf parried the stroke or was felled" resolves itself into "The nimble son of Wonred was not able to return the old soldier's stroke but he (Ongentheow) first carved the helmet so that he... fell," *i.e.* the felling process is analyzed into its parts, a blow on the helmet and the subsequent collapse.

* * * * * * *

As regards the function and meaning of *.ac.*, an outstanding result of the preceding considerations is their confirmation of Schuchardt's protest against the habit of assigning to the word a miscellaneous collection of conjunctional meanings. In so far as such meanings have been assumed without reference to the unity of content which lies behind the antithetic expansion, I am in complete agreement with Schuchardt when he sums up his criticism by saying[2]: "Es sind darum für die Zeit des B. alle spezialisierenden konjunktionalen Bedeutungen zurückzuweisen."

Schuchardt's own conception of the function of *.ac.* I consider doubtful on the score of method. It does not seem to me advisable, in view of our uncertainty about the etymology and original meaning of the word, to start from a theory of its special function in pre-Beowulfian times. All we can know with certainty about *.ac.* at this period is, that it was a particle which played its rôle in the general trend of development from parataxis to greater syntactical unity. When we combine that with the indication that this rôle was restricted in early Anglo-Saxon to the development of the antithetic expansion, we have, I believe, the only safe grounds which can be derived from its history up to the time of *Beowulf*.

In what follows, therefore, I assume no more than that the original expression of an antithetic expansion was an asyndetic succession of main sentences, like "He isn't laughing, he's crying," and that *.ac.* was introduced into the second sentence as a step in the direction of a syntactical unity which would correspond to the underlying unity of content. It is obvious that as long as the antithetic expansion remained such and was not converted into something else, the greatest degree of syntactical unity which it could attain would be represented by two co-ordinate sentences connected by a co-ordinating conjunction.

When a particle is introduced into the second sentence of a parataxis for purposes of unification, it has, firstly, the function of

---

[1] Cp. above, p. 161.
[2] *Die Negation im Beowulf*, p. 74.

an adverb and, secondly, a reference to the preceding sentence[1]. Such particles acquire their syndetic force in different ways. For our purposes it seems advisable to single out two classes of these. The adverb might denote (*a*) a relation between the contents of the sentences as wholes, (*b*) a relation between constituent ideas of these contents. These are exemplified by two types which may be used in Modern English to express an antithetic expansion. Thus I might say "It is not so; *in fact*, it is the opposite," where the adverb stresses the contrast between "It is so" and "It is the opposite" as false and true statements. Or I might say "It is not so; on the *contrary*, it is the opposite," where the adverb stresses the contrast between "so" and "the opposite." It will be noticed that, where the wholes are co-ordinate, the relations between them cannot be very characteristic, hence the second type of reference will have more individualizing and binding force than the first. If, as Schuchardt assumed, *.ac.* had in *Beowulf* the function of an affirmative particle (like German *ja*) felt to stand in correspondence with the preceding negative particle, then the word can only have belonged to our class (*a*) above, and its effect on the two sentences cannot have been more than a first step towards syntactic unity. This seems to be contradicted by the limitation of its use to what, as I have shown, is a particular case of the succession of negation and affirmation. Such limitation, I believe, may be accepted as a sign that the word was felt as characterizing this particular type of succession in a manner more or less clear. In other words, *.ac.* must have belonged to the second of the above classes; it must have had a function more or less individualized by its close association with some characteristic feature of the content.

This association might arise in two ways; either by the word having a specific meaning which, so to speak, *covered* the characteristic relation underlying the antithetic expansion (cp. our *on the contrary*); or, as a consequence of the progressive tendency towards unification, by which a word originally belonging to class (*a*) might develop the function of class (*b*). The latter seems the more likely in the case of *.ac.*, which nothing shows to have been more than a mere form-word. But this form-word starting out from *one* function as an adverb might easily have assimilated others to itself from the context in which it was used. I conceive therefore a sort of syncretic function, the result of the fusing of different elements in one, as that pertaining to *.ac.* A parallel would be the Modern English *but* when used in the expression of an antithetic expansion, for this word has no outstanding meaning

[1] Cp. Brugmann, *Kleine Vergleichende Grammatik*, III, § 891.

of its own and its function seems to include more than one element of relation, to suggest contrast of form as well as contrast of content. Was *.ac.* therefore a real conjunction (of course, co-ordinating, not sub-ordinating)? I do not venture to decide. The question of its exact function hinges on the question "How far had the development from parataxis to syntactical unity proceeded?" The answer does not depend on merely grammatical but also on stylistic considerations—and no one will expect me to enter into these in an Appendix.

APPENDIX IV

ADDITIONAL NOTES ON *FORÞRINGAN* AND *FORWYRNAN*

1. *forþringan*

THERE is one certain occurrence of *forþringan* in a translation from the Latin. By a singular fatality, however, the original is not literally rendered at this place, with the consequence, that it is necessary once more, as it was above (pp. 41 ff.), to *construct* a meaning for the word from its own formal indications and the context. This comes out in the following:

At the beginning of Cap. LXIII of the *Regula Sancti Benedicti* we find provisions: (1) that the brethren should attend church services in a fixed order of precedence; (2) that precedence should *not* be according to age, but (3) should be determined by the date of entry into the monastery[1]. The second of these is worded: "et in omnibus omnino locis etas non discernatur in ordine nec preiudicet." The last two words are rendered in the Anglo-Saxon version (ed. Schröer, p. 115, l. 6): *ne seo ylde þa geogoðe ne forþringe.* The original plainly means: "nor shall age prejudge," or "predetermine," sc. the order of precedence. Since *forþringe* takes an object whose Latin equivalent cannot be supplied with "preiudicet," it obviously means something different from the Latin verb. For this we might assign either of two alternative explanations, which are suggested by the interpolation of *þa geogoðe*:

1. For the provision contained in "nec preiudicet" the translator may have substituted its effect.

Of course, in the abstract, there are two possible consequences, and "nec preiudicet" might convey: "Age shall not prejudge the order of precedence in favour of *either* the older *or* the younger men." As the context shows, we can reject the latter of these alternatives. The translator must have understood: "Age shall not prejudge the matter to the detriment of the younger men" (*i.e.* in favour of the older).

2. The translator may have taken "preiudicet" with the post-classical sense of "praeiudic(i)are," *i.e.* "do prejudice to, injure." In this case, again, he only considered the effect on youth, and

---

[1] A decision of the abbot, and "vitae meritum," could also influence the matter.

thus arrived directly at the sense: "Age shall not be detrimental to youth," sc. with regard to its position in the order of precedence.

We thus see that, whichever sense he gave to "preiudicet," the translator was in a position to understand: "Youth shall not suffer" as the sense of the Latin. But in this context the idea of suffering is obviously limited to privation of a specific kind, namely, to loss of place in order of precedence. What he had in mind was, therefore, that youth was not to be deprived of its rightful place. If he conceived this quite concretely, it may have taken the form in his mind: "Old men shall not deprive young men of their proper place" (this is possible because, of course, *ylde* can mean either "age, time of life" or "old age"). But this does not make it necessary to assume that he used *ylde* here in a sense different from what it has in the preceding clause, where it translates "etas": his own age may, of course, be detrimental to a young man, may deprive him of advantages he would enjoy if he were older; and the preceding *ne sy endebyrdnes be nanre ylde gefadod* shows that the translator clearly realized "etas" as meaning "period of life."

The narrow circle of clearly defined ideas which make up the context, consequently leaves little possibility of doubt that *forþringe* must here express privation; not, however, in a general sense, but in the limited sense that may be defined as "loss of place, position." The passage, therefore, does not guarantee that *forþringan* actually had such vague, general meanings as "keep, or put, down; oppress; crush" (cp. note in Klaeber's edition of *Beowulf*, pp. 166–7). Thus, we might indeed translate: "nor shall age keep youth down"; but this is only because, in *this* context, the translation would bear the meaning: "nor shall age assign youth a lower place than it merits." Naturally, there are a good many different English words which could metaphorically express "loss of position"; but the only means we here have of making a choice, is to take into account the indications afforded by the formal elements of *forþringan*.

The simple verb *þringan* may by itself mean "oppress, afflict," but, as we have seen, this is too general to fit into the context; we are therefore limited to the concrete sense of the simple verb, and this gives us "press, push, or force, out of place," as the only meaning of *forþringan* really justified by the passage under consideration. Even "to crowd out" (German "verdrängen") is too comprehensive, for it suggests "supplant," and this would only be correct, if we were compelled (which, as noted above, is not the case) to give *ylde* the sense of "advanced age." We thus arrive at the following translation of *ne seo ylde þa geogoðe ne forþringe*, viz. "nor shall its period of life displace youth from its position," sc. in order of precedence. Youth's position, be it remarked, is already fixed in the translator's mind by the principle of the third provision mentioned above (p. 166), for this principle is anticipated at the very beginning, in the opening sentence of the chapter. Hence he could easily conceive, that this position, already determined, was something of which youth was not to be deprived by the operation of the opposite principle.

This result agrees with the explanation of *forþringan* as a synonym of *oþþringan* given above (Essay, p. 43), since there is no reason *a priori* why the former, like German "abdrängen," which has an analogous meaning, should not take a double construction, *i.e.* either accusative of the thing plus dative of the person, or accusative of the person plus (if necessary) adverbial enlargement of place. The attempts made to excise the first of these constructions from *Beowulf*, ll. 1084–85*a*, I need not discuss, since they are rebutted by the arguments in my Essay which go to prove that *wea-laf* cannot have a personal reference.

The passage in the *Ormulum* (l. 6169) where the languishing prisoner is described as *Forrbundenn & forrþrungenn* is indecisive. Possibly *forrþrungenn* here means "oppressed"; it may also well mean "cast out of society, rejected, deserted."

2. *forwyrnan.*

In my discussion of l. 1142 (pp. 93 ff. above), I omitted to say anything about the (slight) formal difficulty raised by the omission of a dative of the person, such as is usual with *forwyrnan* (cp. note in Klaeber's edition, p. 170).

There seem to be two possibilities, as follows:

(1) Since Hengest certainly *wanted* to take revenge, the poet may have conceived him as not refusing the universal obligation to himself. Thus, to denote lack of self-restraint, we may say "He can't refuse himself anything."

(2) Since a reminder of revenge is brought to Hengest from the members of the Danish band, the meaning may be: "He did not refuse the universal obligation to his followers."

In either case there is no difference in the result: if Hengest recognizes the obligation for his followers (which could be the only meaning of not refusing it to them), he must, as their leader, recognize it for himself; and *vice versa*.

POSTSCRIPT

(Verbs of Motion)

During proof-reading, Mr Belfour has drawn my attention to the desirability of explaining that my inclusion of *licgan*, *sittan*, and *standan* in the class of primary verbs of motion (above, p. 41) is not meant to convey that these verbs do not also belong elsewhere, namely, to the class of verbs of rest.

My object was to *concede* that the *standan* group may be regarded as allied in meaning to the *faran* group, in so far, namely, as the ideas expressed by *licgan, sittan, standan* may be conceived in two aspects: either, as *rest* in a position, or, as *movement* ending in that position. What I so conceded not only holds in theory for all three verbs, but also applies to Anglo-Saxon usage with regard to *sittan* and *standan*, as Sievers has shown (cp. *PBB.* xii, p. 197 f.). Of course, if we took these three words as mere verbs of rest, there would be little *a priori* justification for a comparison between *forstandan* and *forþringan*; but I desired to show *a posteriori*, that, however we take them, this comparison is of small avail.

LIST of BOOKS and PERIODICALS REFERRED to WITHOUT FULL TITLES

I. BOOKS

VON BAHDER, K. Die Verbalabstracta in den germanischen Sprachen ihrer Bildung nach dargestellt. Halle, 1880.

BERTELSEN, H. Þiðriks Saga af Bern. Udgivet...ved Henrik Bertelsen. 2 vols. Copenhagen, 1905–11.

CHAMBERS, R. W. Beowulf with the Finnsburg Fragment. Edited by A. J. Wyatt. New edition revised...by R. W. Chambers. Cambridge, 1914.

CHAMBERS, R. W. Beowulf: An Introduction to the Study of the Poem with a Discussion of the Stories of Offa and Finn. Cambridge, 1921.

CHAMBERS, R. W. Widsith. A Study in Old English Heroic Legend. Cambridge, 1912.

DELBRÜCK, B. Synkretismus. Ein Beitrag zur germanischen Kasuslehre. Strassburg, 1907.

GERING, H. Beowulf nebst dem Finnsburg-Bruchstück. Übersetzt und erläutert. Zweite durchgesehene Auflage. Heidelberg, 1913.

GREIN, C. W. M. Sprachschatz der angelsächsischen Dichter. Unter Mitwirkung von F. Holthausen neu herausgegeben von J. J. Köhler. Heidelberg, 1912.

GREIN-WÜLKER. Bibliothek der Angelsächsischen Poesie begründet von Christian W. M. Grein. Herausgegeben von Richard Paul Wülker. Kassel, 1883, etc.

HALL, J. R. CLARK. Beowulf and the Finnsburg Fragment. A Translation into Modern English Prose. London, 1911.

HEUSLER, A. Lied und Epos in germanischer Sagendichtung. Dortmund, 1905.

HEYNE, M. Beówulf...herausgegeben von Moritz Heyne. (Elfte und zwölfte Auflage, bearbeitet von Levin L. Schücking. Paderborn, 1918.)

HOOPS, J. Reallexikon der germanischen Altertumskunde. Unter Mitwirkung zahlreicher Fachgelehrten herausgegeben von Johannes Hoops. 4 vols. Strassburg, 1911, etc.

JESPERSEN, O. Negation in English and other Languages. Copenhagen, 1917.

KLAEBER, F. Beowulf and the Fight at Finnsburg. Edited by Fr. Klaeber. London (D. C. Heath and Company).

KLUGE, F. Nominale Stammbildungslehre der altgermanischen Dialekte. Halle, 1899.

MÜLLENHOFF, K. Beovulf. Untersuchungen über das angelsächsische Epos und die älteste Geschichte der germanischen Seevölker. Berlin, 1889.

NECKEL, G. Edda. Die Lieder des Codex Regius nebst verwandten Denkmälern, herausgegeben von Gustav Neckel. 1. Text. Heidelberg, 1914.

PAUL, H. Grundriss der Germanischen Philologie. Herausgegeben von Hermann Paul. Zweite verbesserte und vermehrte Auflage. Strassburg, 1901, etc.

SCHRÖER, A. Die angelsächsischen Prosabearbeitungen der Benedictinerregel. Herausgegeben von Arnold Schröer. Kassel, 1888.

SCHÜCKING, L. L. Die Grundzüge der Satzverknüpfung im Beowulf. 1. Teil. Halle, 1904.

SIEVERS, E. Der Nibelunge Not, Kudrun. Herausgegeben von Eduard Sievers. Leipzig, 1921.

2. PERIODICALS

American Journal of Philology. Baltimore, 1880 ff.

Anglia. Zeitschrift für englische Philologie. Halle, 1877 ff.

Beiblatt zur Anglia. Halle, 1890 ff.

Beiträge zur Geschichte der deutschen Sprache und Litteratur. Original Editors: Hermann Paul and Wilhelm Braune. Halle, 1874 ff. [PBB.]

Bonner Beiträge zur Anglistik, herausgegeben von M. Trautmann.

Englische Studien. Organ für englische Philologie. Leipzig, 1877 ff.

Journal of English and Germanic Philology. Bloomington, Ind. 1897 ff.

Modern Philology. Chicago, 1903 ff.

Publications of the Modern Language Association of America. Baltimore, 1884 ff.

Yale Studies in English, edited by Albert S. Cook. New York (Henry Holt and Company).

Zeitschrift für deutsches Altertum. Original Editor: Moriz Haupt. Leipzig, 1841 ff. [Zs. f. d. A.]

Zeitschrift für deutsche Philologie. Original Editors: E. Höpfner and J. Zacher. Halle, 1869 ff. [Zs. f. d. Ph.]

www.ingramcontent.com/pod-product-compliance
Ingram Content Group UK Ltd.
Pitfield, Milton Keynes, MK11 3LW, UK
UKHW042153280225
455719UK00001B/307